TWEEDHOPE SHEEP DOGS

Best Wishes
Viv Billingham.

By the same author
ONE WOMAN AND HER DOG
THE SHEPHERD'S WIFE

Viv Billingham

TWEEDHOPE SHEEP DOGS

Including a collection of stories and
poetry indicative of shepherding
in the Scottish Borders

Published by Viv Billingham
Tweedhopefoot
Tweedsmuir
Peebleshire

Typeset in 10 on 12pt Times by Annandale Press Services, Moffat.
Origination by Annandale, Press Services.
Cover design by Paul Minns

ISBN: 0-9516515-0-1

Printed in Great Britain by BPCC Wheatons Ltd, Exeter

To my mother, Mabel, and Geoff jnr.

Contents

Acknowledgements

Cover photograph: Harvey Wood. Page 10: *Southern Reporter*. Page 22: *Daily Record*. Page 26: Jack Frazer. Page 29: R. Clapperton. Page 32: Jim and Mira Sharpe. Page 76: *Scottish Farmer*. Page 88: Mr Thin. Page 120: *Scottish Farmer*. Page 132: BBC. Page 166: Mr Thin. Page 180: National Galleries of Scotland. Page 190: Nicholas Servian. Page 196 J. Arthur Dixon.

J. Bain, sign-writer; K. Billingham, Northampton; Borders Regional Council; Countryside Commission for Scotland; J. Dalgliesh, contractor, Moffat; B.P. and S. Foskett, Rockhill Guest House, Moffat; N. Hill, Douglas; J. Long, builder, Moffat; Scottish Tourist Board; B. Toovey, BBC Scotland; Royal Bank of Scotland; N. Wilson, Lochar Publishing, Moffat, and S. Wilson, Walk the Scottish Way, Moffat.

Preface

by Jean Maxwell-Scott and Patricia Maxwell-Scott

Living as we do at Abbotsford, a house that is full of memories of Sir Walter Scott — and his many dogs of all shapes and sizes, it is a great joy to read Viv Billingham's latest book about Tweedhopefoot, telling of her experiences there with both her family and her clever sheep dogs. This is a truly wonderful story of country lore, plus the skill of training Border collies with the necessary patience and consideration for their welfare; there is history and humour too.

Viv and Geoff's 13 eventful years in the Bowmont Valley instilled a great love and knowledge of the Scottish Borderland in both of them and her books must read like a fairy story to those who have to live in a city. How Sir Walter Scott would have enjoyed meeting the Billinghams and their dogs — and how he would have admired their courage in taking on such a major enterprise as 'Tweedhope Sheep Dogs'.

We trust that a great many people will enjoy this book, and like ourselves will wish Viv and Geoff every success in their unusual venture.

Abbotsford
Melrose
Scotland

Foreword
by Jane Roxburghe

Many people tend to take the countryside and the things which happen in it for granted. Viv Billingham's rich and vivid description of her life however, weaves a warm, humorous and sometimes sad tapestry, which cannot fail to strike an instant chord in those of us who already love the countryside and in particular, the Scottish Borders.

Hill farming is very demanding physically and mentally, but however arduous, the fascination of working with animals never palls

Viv and Geoff's contribution to the farming world, with the enthusiastic love of all they do with people, dogs, sheep, (not forgetting the ducks!), has made them friends and admirers world-wide, and it is typical of Viv's generosity to write this enchanting record of her, and her family's life, so that we, as well as our children should benefit.

Children and animals are a natural equation, and as a mother of three, living in a country home already inhabited by three spoilt longdogs, my children have already added three pet lambs, several fish, budgies, hens, ducks, and I am currently resisting a pet pig as the ponies don't like them! Now having read this book, I daily expect a demand for that uniquely intelligent animal, the Border collie, which has been written about in these pages with such affection, and above all, respect.

Cherrytrees, April 1990

Jane Roxburghe

Introduction

One could stay long enough watching the hide-and-seek of cloud shadows on the hills that for me, at least, are like turning the pages of its story. Joy and sorrow chase each other through the years, and the only things that remain constant are the hills and the plaintive ripple of water.

George Burnett, *Companion To Tweed.*

It's happening again, a quenchless desire to put pen to paper is burning within. Descriptive sentences are forever forming inside my head, impatiently jostling for analysis before alarmingly expanding into lengthy paragraphs, as my eager four-footed companions, namely the dogs and I, avidly explore windswept woodland trails that abound throughout these now lonely hills.

I have been far too long away from my writing. Our flit last December, it seems so many moons ago, followed by a sunny hectic spring that led hastily into a damp though somewhat rewarding summer, left few spare moments for the gathering of thoughts. Now thankfully, in the peaceful lull of fast approaching winter the pace of life has slackened to a mere trickle and I can begin the enjoyable task of conversing on paper, the stimulus provided by the ever changing beauty of the surrounding countryside.

The actual setting down comes easy. Imagination coupled with an embarrassing sensitivity are helpful ingredients; however, to my chagrin, both spelling and punctuation require additional vetting and pruning with each approaching year, to the extent that I am on occasion, sorely tempted to find some other means of recreation.

Fortunately, of recent, I've discovered an object that at least provides some measure of encouragement — a tattered autograph album I had brandished as a child, the first page of which enthuses:

Errors like straws upon the surface flow.
Ye who seek pearls must search below.

On turning to the back of the book the final paragraph suggests despairingly that, 'What can't be cured must be endured!'

Most of what I write is drafted in the wee sma' hours, long before daylight. The material is written and rewritten at least five times before being considered legible. The final manuscript is then typed on an ancient typewriter purchased in a sale, the latter task being accomplished in the long winter evenings, for during the daytime I am kept far too busy with the household chores and the schooling of young sheep dogs.

Before we came here my office consisted of a small, extremely cramped space, behind the living room couch. Since settling in at Tweedhopefoot I have escalated to the dizzy heights of an accommodating table. The somewhat stimulating atmosphere (if one can call it that) remains. Garry, the resident OAP collie, snores gently in front of a blazing log fire, blissfully unaware of our kitten's teasing antics. My husband and son continue their banterings, covering a wide variety of topics, whilst the television blares above the clatter of my typewriter.

At this present moment in time, strange though it may seem, I feel far more at ease in these somewhat distracting surroundings; safe within the bosom of my small family. Of late we seem to have travelled a considerable distance in a remarkably short space of time. After what seemed an eternity caring for the flocks of others, both in-bye and out, we have finally realised a life-long ambition in the purchase of our own farm, situated close to the source of the River Tweed. We had for a number of years been invited to demonstrate our sheep dog handling skills at various venues throughout the region. Happily, we are now in a position to provide this service at home, utilising a natural rugged environment of rolling hills and mountain scenery.

I was born shortly after the Second World War and christened Vivien Maybelle Parkes. My place of birth, according to the wording on the certificate was Billingham, in the north-east of England. At the time, my father, William Weldon Parkes, was serving as a Second Mate in the Merchant Navy. My mother is down as Mabel Parkes, formerly Woolley. My destination, had I known, would appear to be hinted at in this very document.

Father was descended from the Macleans, sheep farmers on the Isle of Mull. My mother's family on the maternal side, were from Wales. Her grandfather worked as head gardener on Lord Delamere's estate.

At around the age of four I was taken by my mother to a sheep dog trial held near Norton Green, where the sight of tall shepherds working their clever collies was to create an everlasting impression. From that day onwards I couldn't wait to grow up and become a shepherdess.

Throughout my childhood, father's occupation necessitated that we travelled and, fortunately for me, we lived in the country where I found time both after school and during the holidays to help with the sheep on nearby farms. At Driffield in Yorkshire, my mentor was a kindly shepherd who journeyed to his widespread flock on a bicycle, leading his collie bitch, Jess, on a piece of binder twine. His name was Stan Merrit. I give Stan and Jess the most credit for inspiring me further in my chosen career.

I left school at the age of 15, working first of all on hill farms in Yorkshire and in Wales where I gained valuable experience with both sheep and dogs.

In the early sixties I was employed as a lamber by Mr Ernest Crisp at East Garmondsway, near Sedgefield. I originally went there for six weeks, but stayed on as his shepherd for 12 happy years, living with him and his wife, who cared for me like their own. My proudest achievement during that period being when my flock of mule ewes came second in a national lambing competition with an average of 12 lambs over 200%. It was around this time that I began competing in sheep dog trials with a determined cross-eyed dog called Shep and it was at such an event that I met Geoff Billingham, my husband-to-be. Fortunately we both shared a mutual ambition, to become hill shepherds in the Scottish Border region, where the Border collie evolved.

This we were fortunate enough to achieve several years later, when accompanied by our baby son, Geoff jnr, we flitted along with our worldly goods and menagerie of dogs, cats and hens to scenic Bowmont Water, six miles outside the village of Yetholm and some 12 miles from Kelso. We were to remain in this idyllic situation for 13 years herding lively south country Cheviot sheep, on both the Whitelaw and Swindon hills. During that time we were able to build up a reputation overseas, as well as competing in trials at national and international level. My husband's engraved shepherds' crooks were in demand world-wide and I had written two books describing our life-style.

In view of the insecurity of our occupation we decided to try to find a suitable location where we might endeavour to preserve what we had come to believe is a dedicated and rewarding way of life, as well as sharing our interests and skills with others.

It was an enormous step on our part. The fact that many of our contemporaries had recently become unemployed due to afforestation, spurred us on.

We discovered Tweedhopefoot quite by accident. It is situated on a major scenic tourist route, far enough from the road so as not to endanger our animals. This fact alone was sufficient enough to encourage us to try to purchase the property. The farm's acreage we surmised, would provide a perfect environment in which the dogs could display their natural skills and there was a derelict cottage as well as a useful range of buildings, which would suffice for the time being as kennels. What is reputed to be the smallest school in Scotland, built towards the end of the last century and badly in need of renovation, was also situated on the property. The farm appeared ideal for our purpose and I immediately fell in love with it.

Following what can only be described as strenuous negotiations, much to our great delight, 'Tweedhope Sheep Dogs' has progressed from a wishful dream into reality as one by one, the jig-saw pieces that had been floating in mid-air, have begun to come together. Of course we realise that there is still a long way to go and there is always the possibility that we may fail. We console ourselves with the knowledge that at least we will know the satisfaction of endeavour, for as the well-known saying goes, 'nothing ventured nothing gained'.

Viv Billingham,
Tweedhopefoot
Autumn, 1987

Geoff and Viv with their dogs

1
TWEEDHOPEFOOT

When he was a young man of around 16 summers, my husband, Geoff, was employed as a gamekeeper's boy, on the Hertfordshire estate of H.J. Joel, at Childwickbury. Of the well-known racehorse, gold and diamond mine owner, my husband recalls that not only was he a gentleman but he was also a considerate employer who was treated with great respect by all who knew him.

H.J., as he was affectionately known, rode around his estate on a white pony. He kept a white alsation at each of his studs and should anyone attending a shoot accidentally maim or kill a pheasant of that hue, they were never invited again.

In particular, my husband remembers an employee responsible for taking care of the pumphouse. The man took great pride in his job, keeping the premises immaculate and polishing the brasswork until it shone. He travelled to work each day riding an ancient bicycle. One morning he met up with H.J., who remarked that the machine was looking the worse for wear. He enquired if the man owned another and was told that, unfortunately, he did not. Within the space of a week a brand new bicycle was delivered to his door.

Brenda was a blind semi-retired labrador, living on the estate. She belonged to one of the underkeepers who was away fighting in the war. On a shooting day H.J. insisted that she came along for an airing and never failed to show his appreciation when she returned successfully from my husband's command: 'Hi lost.'

The headkeeper on the estate was nicknamed 'Gillie' Potter, after a comedian on the wireless. My husband was given strict instructions by him, that if in the company of a lord a bird got up, he must show his respect by calling out: 'Cock up my lord.' The thought of that utterance even to this day, fills him with amusement.

In the absence of the underkeepers, a notable worthy known as, 'Old Alf' Price, took care of the gun dogs, game birds and poultry, as well as taking my husband under his wing. One day Potter informed Alf that he was to be replaced by a younger man. This greatly distressed the old chap who doubted if he would find employment elsewhere and dreaded leaving his cottage. After several sleepless nights, he plucked up the courage to explain his anxieties to H.J., who immediately gave him back his job.

My husband had occasion to visit Mr Joel quite recently, and although the estate at Childwickbury has been broken up, his warmth and kindliness — at the wonderful age of 95 years, was still very much in evidence. Little did Geoff realise that some 45 years after leaving Hertfordshire, the so-called wheel of fortune was to turn the full circle.

In September of 1983, after 10 years with the same employer, my husband was informed that due to a reduction in staff he was to be made redundant. Eventually, due to a change in farm policy, he was reinstated. There then followed what can only be described as three insecure years. Finally, in May of 1986, after a great deal of consideration, he informed the management of his resignation.

At that time shepherding jobs were few and far between, and practically none existent if you were over 40 years of age. So there we were, living in a tied house with no options to choose from. In the months that followed accommodation was offered, but it proved unsuitable from the point of view of the dogs. Numerous positions of employment were applied for. We waited in vain for a favourable reply.

Throughout all of this my faith never wavered. I am a great believer that as one door closes another door opens.

Earlier, we had received an invitation to judge two American sheep dog trials, known as the Blue Ridge and Oatlands, near Washington DC. This would be my second trip whereas Geoff would be visiting the United States for the first time. Pat and Pete, two friends of many years standing, offered to take care of things while we were away — namely young Geoff and the dogs.

I experienced my usual misgivings regarding the flight, whilst my husband amazed me with his enthusiasm, insisting on taking the window seat so that he could observe the take-off. Travelling with us was an ornate shepherd's crook, commissioned as first prize for the Oatlands trial. Imagine our pleasure when the crook was eventually received by Lewis Pulfer from Ohio, who won the trial when I was judging the previous year. In view of the hot weather and unco-operative sheep, Lewis and his dog proved themselves true professionals in every sense of the word.

Conditions in some parts of the States being far from favourable, both handlers and especially their dogs, have to struggle for what they achieve with the result that many of our most determined bloodlines are being exported there to the detriment of the breeding programme in this country.

Oatlands proved to be a truly magnificent estate. The mansion house is set in acres of fertile parkland, six miles south of Leesburg, in the state of Virginia — and it was

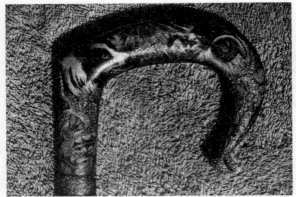

*An ornate
shepherd's crook*

The presentation

here that Candy Kennedy, one of America's top lady handlers, introduced me to sloe gin, a particularly powerful pick-me-up, or knock-me-down, depending on which way you care to look at it.

Built in the year 1800, Oatlands belongs to the National Trust for Historic Preservation. The mansion house is open to the public and stands amidst formal terraced gardens. It was at one time at the centre of a 3400-acre plantation. Surrounded by giant boxwood trees, magnolias and many other spectacular species, it commands a sweeping view of northern Virginia's renowned hunt country. The interior provides a perfect setting for displaying an extensive collection of British, French and American antique furniture.

In a previous journal I told of two American sisters, Ariana and Alana, who paid a visit to Bowmont Water during a severe snow storm. They have since become firm friends. Ariana lives with her author husband, Ralph, and two children, in a charming olde worlde cottage with a thatched roof, near Oxon.

Alana lives in Washington and whilst we were there she was endeavouring to form her own company. She drives a vintage car with 'real' leather upholstery and before we could say 'President Roosevelt', we were uplifted and borne away to stay at the home of her mother, Gilliace Giberza. A VIP trip around the White House was arranged for us by Alana's sister, Lilibet, who worked there and on arrival at the impressive home of the President, until then only seen by us on television, we were whisked away to a side-entrance escorted by an armed guard. We were then guided through a series of locked apartments until finally just when we were about to give up any hope of ever seeing the light of day we arrived at our final destination — the

Geoff and Viv in Washington DC

front of a long queue! Geoff was dressed in his best and looking like a country gentleman while I wore my pink silk, crowned with a wide-brimmed straw hat bedecked with dried flowers and a long pink ribbon. The crowd stared agog. I don't know who they imagined we were. Their curiosity was, however, short-lived; when the main door opened to admit us, the conducted tour progressed at such a speed that we were almost trampled underfoot.

Eventually, we managed to catch our breath as everyone crowded to the window, (leaving our muscular guide addressing thin air) — eagerly waving to the President who was about to take off in his big red helicopter.

Washington is impressive to say the least, a clean city exhibiting great colonial charm. The roads are spacious, shaded by avenues of stately trees and the towering cathedral is a must for every visitor. Both early and late, joggers of all shapes, sizes and cultures are very much in evidence, giving one the impression that Americans are extremely health conscious.

Alana had been busy on our behalf arranging a meeting with a senior executive of the National Geographic Society, who had been a friend of her late father. This meeting proved lucrative in that in due course it was arranged that they would send over a producer to make a television documentary featuring our sheep dogs. Paul Gasek was their choice, a tall, funny and sensitive man very much a professional in his field.

Permission was obtained for filming to take place at Floors Castle, Kelso, where we had agreed previously to stage a sheep and duck herding demonstration in aid of a well-known charity. On that day we were presented to Her Royal Highness the Duchess of Kent, patron of the charity, who looked as attractive and elegant as she is portrayed on

Oatlands: The winners

television. Although our day at Floors went well, the film shot there proved unsuitable because the movement of the dogs and ducks was too fast for the camera to follow. On returning home the ducks completely took me by surprise and flew away down the valley. Thank goodness they remained 'grounded' during the demonstration!

To our dismay and Paul's, all manner of disasters plagued the actual shooting. The weather for a start was far from what it might have been, and because of it, a real-life tragedy occurred practically on our doorstep when a friend and neighbour, Dr Robin Armstrong, was washed away by a flash flood and drowned. A few days later an elderly shepherd, Bob Fraser, perpetrator of the famous 'Mindrum' line of Border collies, collapsed and died at a trial we were attending. Paul was clearly upset and suggested abandoning filming for that day. I persuaded him that it was the last thing Bob would have wanted. He had led a long and happy life doing the things he enjoyed most, namely being a shepherd and competing with his dogs at trials. He had on this occasion completed a good course before leaving the field, content with his run. My immediate sympathy lay with his friends of many years standing. People like kindly Willie Scott, the most sought after time-keeper on the trial circuit; Alan Rogerson, who calls himself 'the last of the roaring 'herds'; Adam Hindmarsh, well past the age of retirement but as straight as a ramrod, and last but by no means least, another character whose name escapes me; he sang umpteen verses of 'Bellingham Fair' for Paul's enjoyment and eventually restored happy smiles to sombre faces. I suggested a dram and we each raised our glass as a final salute 'to absent friends'.

Because we were no longer employed, the relevant scenes in the film had to be created elsewhere. Joe

Her Royal Highness, the Duchess of Kent

McRobert, a fellow shepherd known as 'Big Joe', fortunately came to our rescue, with the result that the filming
was completed successfully, leaving a satisfied Paul free to
explore pastures new. He has kept in touch and informs us
that the resulting work — entitled *A Shepherd and
Shepherdess* — went down well in the States where it has
been shown to millions of Americans on more than one
occasion.

It was while completing the programme at Fingland,
where 'Big Joe' herds, that two properties shortly coming
up for sale were pointed out.

They were Badlieu, consisting of eight rough acres and a
tiny yellow cottage which reminded me of a pat of butter,
and one mile away, the picturesque steading with the
romantic name of Tweedhopefoot, set in 80 riverside acres,
which on this particular occasion were barely visible in the
rolling mist.

Badlieu, being the closest, was the first property we
explored. Joe beckoned me across the burn and among the
bracken fronds revealed a faithful collie's final resting place
marked by a stone that had been engraved long ago by an
appreciative master. Inside the cottage the rooms were less
spacious than those of our present home which would mean
parting with some of our furniture, plus bits and pieces
carefully collected over the past 15 years from salerooms
and through inheritance. Geoff was entirely more enthusiastic, the price was not out of the way and it wouldn't take
much of an effort to make it habitable, he enthused.
Reluctantly I found myself agreeing, while in reality my
heart lay halfway up the glen.

The occupants, Jim and Mira Sharpe, kindly showed us
around Tweedhopefoot, our next port of call. Jim had
worked in the surrounding forest before he retired, planting

acre upon acre of young trees on the steep hillsides. The cottage and land went with the job. It had recently been put on the market by its owners, Fountain Forestry. Jim and Mira were shortly moving to a new home in nearby Tweedsmuir; they were leaving behind a beautifully tended flower garden hewn out of poor soil, and many happy memories.

From the moment I stepped out of the car into the farmyard, I felt completely at home. Above all, I sensed that here, amidst the peaceful hills, was security and space to develop and put down roots. Most important, here was an opportunity to preserve and share a dedicated way of life, that of the hill shepherd, his collie dogs, stone-walling, stick-dressing and the hand-shearing of sheep, all of which are dying arts.

We returned from our visit to the United States in the middle of June and in order to keep the wolf from the door we set ourselves up as booksellers, spending most of our days travelling around the villages and towns in our area selling my latest book *The Shepherd's Wife*. I had published this second effort myself. Fortunately, both my books obtained a lot of publicity in the press and on television. Because of this we received hundreds of orders from readers, bookshops and libraries. These orders we parcelled in the evenings. It is surprising how clumsy hands, better suited to catching sheep, soon became adept at this time-consuming task.

For most of our lives we had rattled around like peas in a drum owning one old banger after another. Our mode of transport at this particular time was, much to our consternation, beginning to show advanced signs of wear and tear. Money from the book was coming in steadily. On the strength of this, and because our livelihood depended on it, we decided to invest in a younger more reliable model. I strongly suspect that it was also a means of uplifting our sagging spirits, for in our minds, even though a new shepherd had been employed, our responsibilities still lay with the flock on the hill that we had taken care of for the past 13 years. Our sympathy, with our energetic collie dogs, cooped up inside gloomy kennels.

I bought several publications in order to scour the cars for sale adverts. 'Immaculate' in many cases meant touched up, or re-sprayed, and the term 'average mileage', over and above what one would expect. One afternoon in late June whilst on our way to deliver books, we were driving past a garage, when I espied parked on the forecourt, resplendent in the summer sun, my dream car, a gleaming silver coupe whose masculine lines as far as I was concerned positively oozed reassurance. We stopped to take a look, knowing full well the car would be beyond our means. The mileage was low, the bodywork immaculate and the powerful engine as clean as a whistle. Its one previous owner, had been transported in sheer luxury for under two years.

Geoff checked all the relevant information while I secretly mooned over the blue crushed velvet upholstery, stereo and heated front seats. We were asked if we would care to go for a test drive. Practicality prevailed, and we enquired of the selling price. The car was, as we expected, way beyond our present means. After thanking the proprietor we scrambled disconsolately back into 'Mad Max' and chugged off into the sunset, consoling ourselves with 'better the devil you know'.

Three weeks passed, before purely by chance we found ourselves once again in the vicinity of 'the dream car'. 'Let's see if it's still there,' I persuaded hopefully. 'If it is, they may accept a lower offer,' I cajoled. Geoff junior was present on this occasion. 'You can't do that mum,' he retorted, in shocked tones. 'And if you do I'm not coming with you,' muttered his father.

I deposited them both in a nearby hotel and 10 minutes later after persuading the garage owners to drop the price by £600, I returned with the good news that the car was ours. Within minutes we were standing alongside. 'You can't put dogs in there,' stated father, peering critically inside. 'Can I play my cassettes?' enquired young Geoff hopefully.

The car had an automatic gearbox and neither of us had ever driven an automatic before. It was exactly a fortnight before a helpful acquaintance suggested that instead of using both feet we would find it much easier using one. By this time Geoff snr. had knocked together a made-to-measure wooden dog frame and Geoff jnr. had got to play his precious cassettes, not once but many times, whilst I suffered in silence, impatiently clutching my collection of best classical music. The 'new' car considerably boosted our sagging spirits. Perhaps we are on our way at last, I endeavoured to reassure myself, as we purred along in comfort. What a relief not to suffer the constant anxiety of breaking down miles from home, of experiencing essential bits drop off, plus the endless repair bills one regularly receives when owning a geriatric conveyance.

By the month of October we had looked over both Badlieu and Tweedhopefoot. Believing that we had not the slightest chance of purchasing the latter property we had shelved the idea for the time being. The subsequent sale of Badlieu jolted us into action. We made an appointment with our bank manager who, being a banker, naturally had to be cautious. He listened attentively to our ideas and, I believe, in theory approved of them. The next step was to prepare a prospectus. Time was running out as offers for the farm had to be in by the following week. With the help of a friend's son I typed throughout the night while my husband drew up the plans, finishing the document by 5am the following morning.

That same day I approached the Newcastle Building Society with whom I was an investor, to get a mortgage. A surveyor was immediately sent out by them to evaluate the farm cottage. To our relief a mortgage was agreed. We were halfway there. Two days later we returned to the bank and were granted a loan with which to purchase the farmland.

We possessed at that time several thousand pounds. A further small loan from each of our families helped make the purchase possible. Offers for the land had been invited by the estate agents Harrison and Hetherington. Our solicitor lodged ours. There then followed the longest and the most anxious wait of our lives.

It was three o'clock in the afternoon when the telephone rang with the news that Tweedhopefoot and its 80 acres of rough grazing was ours. I didn't know whether to laugh or cry and will always remember the overwhelming feeling of relief that flooded over me as I rushed out of the house and down to the burnside where Geoff was exercising his dogs. 'How does it feel to be a farmer?' I called out excitedly above the roar of the water.

Later that same evening, once the initial reaction of surprise and disbelief had subsided, we quickly returned to earth, appreciating fully the enormous responsibility and debt we had acquired. We were both past the age when life supposedly begins but there was after all, young Geoff to consider — and he did possess an artistic flair as well as an engaging way with both people and animals.

After seriously weighing up both the pros and the cons we came to the conclusion that in taking this enormous leap we had very little to lose and hopefully everything to gain.

THE CANNY SHEPHERD LADDIES O' THE HILLS

Noo there's songs aboot your sodgers
And yer sailors by the score
Of tinkers and of tailors and of
Other men galore
But aal sing ye a wee ditty
Thet ye'v nivver hoord before
Oh the canny shepherd laddies o' the hills.

CHORUS:
O' the shepherds of the Coquet, of the
Alwin and the Rede
The Beaumont and the Breamish
They are aal the same breed
Wi' their collie dog beside them
And their stick wi 'horn heed
That's the canny shepherd laddies o' the hills.

They climb oot amang the heather
Ere it's torned the break of day
Through the bent, amang the moss hags,
And the bogs they wend their way
Quick ta see a sheep that's makeed
Or a tup that's slipped away
That's the canny shepherd laddies o' the hills

Noo they send their dog aroond the sheep
Wi' cries of gan oot wide.
Then they'll whistle wi a note so shrill
Come by, Moss lie doon on the bit,
or aal stick your dusty hide
That's the canny shepherd laddies o' the hills.

If the lambing time be stormy
They will corse and they wull sweer
There's a lamb that's lost its mammy
And ave skinned an ould yow here
There's some hev tekken the sickness
Nae mare trouble can I beer
That's the canny shepherd laddies o' the hills.

At the backend ti the marts they gan
And if the prices are dear
To celebrate they'll treat their pals
To whiskey or tae beer
But if the prices they are bad
It tekkes a dram tae cheer
That's the canny shepherd laddies o' the hills.

If the winter time be stormy
And the drifts are piling high
They nivver fail tae tek the risk
Thet in the sna they might die
They put their sheep into a stell
That they might safely lie
That's the canny shepherd laddies o' the hills.

Noo if ye hev gone as aa hev done
Just ni on twenty yeers
Nay kinder hearted folk yul ivver meet
Though yul travel far and near
The kettles set a boilin' and wi
Cries' just sit down here'
That's the canny shepherd laddies o' the hills.

Noo, we aal torn oot at Aalwinton
Tae see the shepherds show
Then inta Foremans for a drink
We wi wor cronies gan
They'll roar and shout and dance
And sing
But fight' God bless ya' no
That's the canny shepherd laddies o' the hills.

Noo ave sed nae woord aboot
Their wives, for I think there is
Nae need
For in ivvery hoose that aa hev been
Aa think they are the heed
And aa think that yeel agree wi me
It tekkes good wives to breed
The canny shepherd laddies o' the hills.

Northumbrian Shepherd Song

2

LIFE AFTER BOWMONT

Our date of entry into 'Tweedupfit', as it is known locally, was arranged for December 18, 1986. Fortunately, our new neighbour, 'Big Joe', had been entrusted with the key, so we were able to gain access prior to the time stipulated in order to deposit our 'breakables' and the unopened Christmas gifts we had already received.

At last the great day arrived. We were awake and ready at the crack of dawn, anxiously waiting for the enormous cattle wagon that was to transport all our wordly goods except Tarka our shepherding horse, who was coming along later. For the first time in our lives we would be living under our very own roof; the acreage, the river, the view, all of these were an added bonus. It was time to reflect, time to broaden our horizons, time to move on. We had outgrown Bowmont and were ready to exchange one life-style for another. The famous Tweed Valley, steeped as it is in history, is a dream of a place; our new home a fairy tale come true and had I been invited to paint a picture of my idea of heaven — including all the necessary attributes, I would not be able to portray so aptly what nature herself has already generously provided.

Rory, a poet, artist and friend, stayed overnight in order to help with the move. He had latterly been invalided out of the fire service because of an accident and originally visited the Bowmont Valley so that I would sign his copy of my first book.

I was clearing away the last of the breakfast dishes when George, Young of Yetholm's driver, reversed his wagon carefully through the gate and along the drive to the sound of barking dogs. Outside the back door our seven cats and three ducks were already lined up in wooden crates, whilst the dogs waited patiently inside their kennels. They would be the last to be loaded into the already rapidly filling truck. Meanwhile, some 70 odd miles north-west of Yetholm the new inhabitants at Badlieu, a Mr and Mrs Perfect, were already installed, no doubt dreaming of springtime when they would set up business as antiquarian booksellers and transform 'the pat of butter' into a brilliant white des. res. with a welcoming red door.

At long last the wagon was loaded, mirrors skilfully padded with mattresses, and larger heavier pieces of furniture tied down firmly. A truly professional operation performed by George. Strangely, that morning I opened the door to find a family of six chattering magpies had landed on the grass outside, the first that we had seen in the area in the 14 years we had lived there. The birds unexpected appearance brought to mind a childhood rhyme:

One for sorrow, two for joy,
Three for a girl, four for a boy,
Five for silver, six for gold,
Seven for a secret never to be told.

I had agreed to ride in the back of the wagon with our 11 dogs to quell any bickering. A comfortable armchair had been strategically placed there on my behalf. I quickly clambered inside and wrapped myself in a large blanket surrounded by squirming black and white bodies, eagerly wagging rears and puzzled expressions. Once seated the tailboard was hurriedly raised, just in case any of the occupants should have second thoughts and try to escape. A couple of minutes later we were on our way, my husband following in one heavily laden car and Rory and young Geoff in the other. Geoff was sad at losing his school friends and the only home he had ever known. I was sorry to leave the sheep and the scenery, but enormously looking forward to the warm, dry cottage awaiting us in peaceful Peebleshire. There was time for one last fleeting glance at fast receding Bowmont Water through a narrow aperture in the side of the wagon. As we rattled down the familiar winding road I whispered a fond farewell to mighty Cheviot as it disappeared behind round sheep-dotted hills, while pulling the blanket more tightly around my shoulders to keep out winter's chill. I slept for a couple of hours, then pinched myself to keep awake, eagerly awaiting the vibrations that would inform me that we had reached Tweedhopefoot.

Some three hours later we arrived at our destination in a raging blizzard. The dogs, apart from a minor squabble had been well behaved, stretched out at my feet like recumbent crocodiles; their steamy breaths hanging in the air.

As we bumped and shook down the farm track my first view was of dancing white flakes, and the uppermost branches of spruce heavily laden with snow. We reversed up to the gate and the tailboard was quickly lowered. Much to everyone's amusement I half-walked, half-fell out of the wagon. I had completely seized up with the cold whilst I had been asleep. 'Big Joe' was waiting to welcome us with a roaring fire, he immediately telephoned his wife, Moira, who quickly came to the rescue and in no time at all thawed me out with a hot drink. Fortunately most of the carpets had been laid the previous week, so it was just a

My family is complete

matter of carrying in the furniture and making up the beds.
This task was soon accomplished and all of the animals fed
before we tumbled gratefully into bed.

The cottage has a small kitchen, medium sized lounge,
bathroom and three other rooms previously used as
bedrooms. An accommodating loft runs the full length of
the house. This will eventually make a spacious studio with
an uninterrupted view of the Tweed Valley and surrounding
countryside. As you enter the back door there is a cupboard
or small room straight ahead, one wall of which contains a
window that overlooks the farmyard, the wall opposite
backs onto the fireplace in the lounge. Noting that this was
the warmest room in the house young Geoff quickly
commandeered it as his bedroom.

The week that followed was spent polishing, cleaning
and unpacking the bric-a-brac. I was determined that come
Christmas Day everything would be ship-shape and hearty.
It was, but unfortunately I slept through most of the festive
season.

Tarka, our mare, arrived at Tweedhopefoot in time for
Christmas. By then the farm road had become impassable
and she had to be led down it. In order to reassure her I
called out a welcome; at last our family was complete.
After sniffing warily in the doorway of her new stable she
daintily stepped inside, glad of the shelter it provided from
the bitter north-east wind.

Thankfully, none of our animals suffered any ill-effects
after their long journey. The ducks, as soon as they were
released quacked contentedly about the yard. The cats —
Jemima, Silver, Tabby, Sooty, Sweep, Young Rambo and
my beloved long-haired rascal Greystoke — after spending
a couple of days shut in the old cottage eventually found
their way to the back door, where they settled as though

Top: *Duck drive*. Bottom: *Catastrophe*

they had lived there all of their nine lives. Surprisingly, I cannot call myself a lover of cats — the reason being that they decimate the bird population. I do however, admire their independence and affection towards each other. Felines seem to attach themselves to me more than they used to. Can the reason be, that as time passes my lap becomes more ample?

From the very moment their paws touched down on Tweed Valley soil, the dogs, like me, were completely at home. Observing them explore every nook and cranny, their tails waving excitedly, I experienced more than a hint of sadness due to the absence of my husband's old faithfuls, the retired trials brace pair, litter sisters Jed and Trim. If only they could have been among the happy throng, my happiness would have been complete.

Before leaving Bowmont we had the agonising decision of deciding the fate of the devoted pair, then in their sixteenth year. They had followed unquestioning at their master's heels to at least 12 hill lambings, never disputing a command no matter how tedious. They had gained accolades too numerous to mention the length and breadth of Britain, .

Both bitches were fading fast. Trimmy had become so frail that a puff of wind would have blown her over. She had to be lifted in and out of her kennel, her sight and hearing practically none existent. Jed, always the more robust and determined of the pair, was infinitely more alert. However, when parted from her sister for any length of time, she began to fret. We had evidence of this when Trim, suffering a bout of arthritis, spent a few days in the warmth of the kitchen. Jed, eventually discovering her whereabouts, went delirious with delight.

After living and working as one throughout all of their

Geoff with Trim, left, and Jed

lives, their fate was the most difficult decision we have ever been called upon to make. Jed would have possibly gone on a while longer, but after a deal of deliberation, we decided that it was kinder by far to have them both put to sleep together.

They lie beside Pip, Tweed and Jan, other never-to-be-forgotten friends, assured always of a place in our hearts.

Prior to our move into Tweedhopefoot, a squatter had taken up residence, leaving his calling card everywhere. We named him 'Supermouse' for no other reason than, on the few occasions we had observed him, we noted that he was the largest and sleekest rodent of his kind. We were to discover how he had managed to become so gross when young Geoff came to open the Christmas presents. Half of a large bar of chocolate had been completely devoured. 'Supermouse' was to put in several more appearances, one of which almost proved fatal.

It happened when Harry Thomson and his wife Ute, who farm in Sweden, were paying us a visit. We were watching television when suddenly Harry bounded to his feet and with three enormous strides landed in the hall doorway, shouting excitedly: 'There's a mouse!' Everything happened so quickly that we were completely taken by surprise and sat there transfixed. Harry immediately brought down his large foot with a sickening thud. Young Geoff grimaced in horror, fully expecting poor 'Supermouse' to be splattered all over the newly whitened walls. 'I've got 'im by the tail,' yelled Harry jubilantly. My heart sank into my boots. Then, 'lost 'im,' roared Harry disappointedly. My eyes met with young Geoff's as a feeling of relief flooded through both of us.

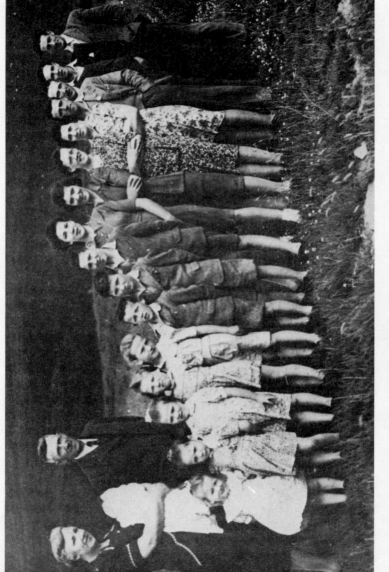

Mr and Mrs McTier and family

Sadly that was the last we saw of 'Supermouse', our squatter-cum-lodger. His near demise proved too much of a close shave and he returned from whence he had come.

On the property, approximately 200 yards away beside the road, stands a tiny school, reputed to be the smallest in Scotland. It is built of corrugated sheets, with a wooden interior. On the roof there is a chimney, but unfortunately the old stove that was installed to provide heating for the children has long since been removed. When we first saw the school, although in a state of disrepair, it was not without character. The building had once provided the gift of education to shepherds' children and although on our land, it belonged to the local education authority, who had placed it under a preservation order. Built a year or two before the turn of the century the school had ceased to be in use by the late 1930s. In 1936 Miss Jean Fleming arrived to teach here. Fifty years later she still lives in the area.

In the 1940s a shepherd named McTeir lived with his wife and 19 children in the other cottage at Tweedhopefoot. It was then that a new cottage, in which we now live, was built.

Mrs McTeir is alive and well and lives today in Moffat.

What a pity that by the time the McTeirs lived at Tweedhopefoot the 'wee school', as it is known, was already closed. However, it did serve for a while as a Sunday school and latterly, as a camp for boys. Because the building was obsolete I wrote to the authorities about renovating it. They were, I'm glad to say, happy to hand over the property to us.

Young Geoff would give anything to be taught there. His present schooling involves a round trip to Peebles of 50 miles. He is collected every morning by mini-bus. On reaching Tweedsmuir his journey then deviates along a winding road to scenic Talla, before connecting with a larger coach at Broughton.

THE WEE SCHOOL
Comprehensive education 30 years ago

The 'academy' was a hut on a bare hillside. But we learned much there — teacher as well as pupils.

                                                J.B. Fleming

Comprehensive Education? What does this mean?

My mind flashes back to the date of my appointment to Tweedhopefoot school, on the Peeblesshire side of the border with Dumfriesshire.

To say I was displeased when I received the letter of appointment would indeed be an understatement. My father had just died. My mother had to be left to live alone. While I was being banished from civilisation. It was like a 'sentence' to me. I was horrified at the thought of being buried in the hills, miles from anywhere, without the possibility of even getting home for a weekend.

Tweedhopefoot was nine miles from Moffat, on the road that goes over the Devil's Beeftub, and just one mile from the source of Tweed. At that time of course, teachers were 10 a penny so I was fortunate to receive an appointment at all. I reckon that at least 75% of my classmates never got teaching posts. To refuse it was just unthinkable, no matter what my feelings were.

In the middle of winter, January 1936, I made my acquaintance with the 'academy' — a small corrugated-iron hut about 10ft by 8ft with a shed and a coal-house attached. It stood alone on the bare hillside, but fortunately near the main road. There was only one house near — that occupied by the shepherd. It was indeed fortunate for me that this family was one of the most hospitable, as I had to obtain lodgings here. There was nowhere else.

No-one could have done more to make the lot of a very lonely young teacher a happy one. I was accepted, and treated as one of the family. The friendship then begun lasts to this day. Whenever I visited the shepherd and his wife after they had retired to Moffat, I received a welcome fit for a queen. They celebrated their diamond wedding two years ago. It was with deep regret that I learned recently that the old man had died. He was well past his four score years.

Tweedhopefoot was the smallest school on the mainland of Scotland at that time. The number of pupils on the roll was four: George, who was 13, and Betty his sister, seven years old, were from the shepherd's cottage at Fingland, one and a half miles away; Neil, who was nine, came over the hills from Earlshaugh, a distance of three miles, and Albert, five, who lived in the cottage near the school.

Lessons started at 10am and finished at 3pm with an hour off for lunch. Three of the children carried a 'piece' and I made cocoa for them. No school lunches in those days! Water had to be carried in an enamel jug from a nearby spring each morning. Hot water from a tap was an unknown luxury. There was no running water in the house either. It had to be pumped with a huge iron hand-pump into a large, yellow earthenware tub.

School toilet facilities were primitive. Two planks over the stream with a little hut on top, which at least provided some protection from the elements, served as a WC, or should I say C, since the W was missing in the toilet. It flowed underneath. We didn't even rise to a chemical closet.

Wee School
around 1900

Facilities may have been poor, but there existed such a comradeship between teacher and pupils as could not be conceived of in a big, modern establishment. There was a thirst for knowledge and a will to work seldom found in such measure in a large class.

Methods, of necessity, had to be individual. All the usual subjects were taught. There were four 'classes' for the basic subjects — reading, arithmetic, English and writing. All other subjects were taken together — Albert and Betty listening eagerly to stories in history or sharing adventures in faraway places with the two older boys in their geography lesson.

Albert had a most vivid imagination and was inspired by events in Scottish history. He sat completely silent and motionless, riding with Bruce to Bannockburn, or hiding with Prince Charlie. Such subjects did not form part of his curriculum at all, of course, but I could not prevent him from listening. Being very bright, he learned as much as the others.

Music was difficult to teach without the use of an instrument and with only one child that could remain in tune. Usually we sang in five 'parts' — the teacher alone keeping the melody and the children providing harmonies (or more often discords) of their own. It may have been dreadful for a listener (had there been any,) but it was none the less enjoyable for the participants. They had quite a repertoire of Scots songs, *The Peat Fire Flame* from Kennedy-Fraser's *Songs of The Hebrides* was a particular favourite.

The response of the children to religious teachings was thoughtful and reverent. Many of their questions on this subject were profound. Naturally enough one of their favourite pieces for praise and repetition was the Twenty

Third Psalm. *The Lord's My Shepherd* really meant something to these shepherds' children.

The four children carried out some first-class projects on their own initiative. This is the method that is now being 'introduced' to schools as something new. One that comes to my mind is a project on wool. It started with the sheep's wool gathered on the hillside. They dyed it with dyes of their own making, they spun it, (albeit very roughly) with an old spindle and they wove it into rough cloth, forming a simple pattern of checks which they had worked out on paper beforehand.

A follow-up visit which I had hoped to pay to a Border tweed mill, to let the children see the whole process of tweed manufacture, did not materialise. The firm did not cater for individual visitors — only parties! The smallest school apparently did not aspire to the proportions of a party. Such visits to industry are the very thing now being advocated in the Report on Primary Education.

Another project from which the children learned a great deal — especially in measurement, calculation and proportion — was the building of a doll's house from match boxes. It did not take so long to collect the boxes as one might imagine. A great many matches were used in the children's homes as there was no electricity — lighting was by oil lamps. The house measured approximately 24in by 18in. It had three rooms, a kitchen and a bathroom and was equipped with furnishings made by the children. It was eventually raffled in aid of a children's charity.

There was no need for me to teach 'nature'. We lived with it. Dinner time, after the 'piece' was eaten, was spent watching the moorland birds, 'guddling' for trout in the burn (they were always put back in), or collecting specimens of wild flowers for our album. In the spawning season children often spent their lunch-time break watching the salmon struggling to the uppermost reaches of the Tweed. Nature was part of our lives.

I remember being out with young Albert one night (he was only five.) It was pretty dark because there was a new moon. A remark I passed about the darkness and the lack of moonlight made him look up into the sky and out came the following utterance: 'There's the moon up there, Miss, but somebody's ta'en a b----- slice oot o' it.'

We never found out where he learned the adjective — certainly not in school or in his own home! In winter, heavy snowfalls prevented three of the pupils from reaching the school for days at a time, and sometimes we didn't see Neil for weeks, as there is no road between Earlshaugh and Tweedhopefoot. This left us with the ideal teacher pupil ratio — one teacher, one pupil. The school was seldom closed for stormy weather as there was always one boy that could reach it — even if it was on the teacher's back!

Although I had been brought up in the country, I had never realised what a severe storm meant in the hills. I have seen the shepherds come in with their clothes so caked with frozen snow that the trousers stood up by themselves when they took them off. I have seen the hair of the dogs so 'balled up' that the poor animals were weighed down to the ground, yelping as they trailed their stomachs across the snow. On one occasion the blizzard was so bad that a shepherd became lost on his own hill which he tramped twice a day. It was only by luck that he came to a well-known landmark and found his way home.

In summer, life in the hills was wonderful. We had lessons out of doors, with not a sound to disturb us but the bleat of the sheep, the song of the birds, and the ripple of the infant river. When lessons in school were over, my lessons began. After a cup of tea with home-made scones spread with home-churned butter, I went off with the shepherd, six miles round the hill. What I didn't know about the sheep at the end of two years wasn't worth knowing, and even if I did fall into a well-covered peat bog occasionally, it was all part of my education.

Talking of peat takes my mind back to the peat-cutting. This was another new experience for me. The sodden peat was cut with a special spade and thrown out to dry. Then it was turned, 'fitted' that is, stood up on end in pairs, 'rickled' (put up in small piles with air spaces between the peats), and finally carted home and stacked for the winter. During the cold season eight pailfuls of peat were burned every night. They burn away very quickly, but what a wonderful thing is a peat fire! Even now I can still smell the peat reek.

We had our regular visits from vagrants, some of whom we could time within a few days. The distance covered by some of these 'gentlemen of the road' was truly amazing. We had one 'regular' who travelled from Cumberland right through the Borders of Scotland, following the Tweed from its source to its mouth at Berwick on Tweed, back to the English side, through Northumberland to start on his rounds again. He would spend a night in the byre and be off the next morning.

I first made his acquaintance when I went to milk the cow one evening. He was a most interesting fellow and could talk intelligently on a variety of subjects. He could not tell me what had made him take to the road in the first place, but he had been on the move for so many years that it had just become his way of life. He carried his Bible in his inside pocket, and told me he often read it as he walked along. After I had talked with him on this particular evening he inquired who I was. On being told by the shepherd's wife that I was 'the teacher', he inquired: 'Is she a certified teacher?'

'Certified' or not, I was truly sorry to leave my home in the hills when, after nearly two years, I received an appointment to a large class of infants in Innerleithen. On looking back, I know I would have missed a very great deal had I not had this experience. What I accepted as a 'sentence' and a challenge turned out to be one of the most interesting periods of my teaching career.

Tweedhopefoot had something to give me that I could not have gained elsewhere. It certainly made my education more comprehensive. I trust that I, in turn, gave something to Tweedhopefoot.

I am afraid that the day of the small school is over. Tweedhopefoot School was closed down six months after I left it, and since then many others in the county have gone. The children had to travel daily to Tweedsmuir, a distance of 12 miles return. After the age of 11 they had to attend Broughton Secondary School, which meant a journey of 26 miles return.

Now, in the name of progress, the axe has fallen on the Secondary Department at Broughton; all children in the upper Tweed Valley have to make a round trip of 50 miles daily to attend Peebles High School.

It may be true that small one-teacher schools are not viable units, to use a modern phrase, but must we measure everything in £.s.d.?

3
THE BUSINESS

*Roads whiles may seem lanesome and braes unco'
steep,
For wi' fates dire decision we're forced to compete.
But the lot of the shepherd who wanders alone
Is whiles to be envied by kings on the throne.*

John Dixon

Following 'the starving' I received in the wagon en route
from our former abode, I developed what can only be
compared to kennel cough. The illness wracked my entire
frame throughout the following five months until a
welcome breath of fresh spring air finally banished it
completely. The memory of the hardship we experienced
during our first year will remain with us always. I survived
on optimism alone learning more in those early months
about the pitfalls of starting a business than I had absorbed
in a multitude of previous casual deals.

Without a doubt, sheer physical effort is to be preferred
to that of mental strain. The constant pressure that occurs
when bombarding one's brain with a barrage of facts and
figures — never mind the associated problems, is not for
the faint-hearted. I believe it was our sense of humour,
though on occasions somewhat diminished, that eventually
carried us through.

It is often stated that money is the root of all evil. One
thing that I learned early on was that instant success in
business, unless one possesses a magical wand, depends
solely on this commodity. No matter how impressive an

idea appears on the drawing board — and I believe our idea at its worst to be original — no matter how much effort one is prepared to expend or the fact that the participants have enjoyed a great deal of publicity; at the end of the day instant success depends on hard cash alone.

After religiously exploring every avenue and pursuing each available opportunity, we finally arrived at the realisation that without capital we were not necessarily on to a loser, rather that our rate of development would be impaired to the extent that we would be in our dotage before we could begin to enjoy the fruits of our labour.

In the past I have oft been accused of looking at life through rose-coloured spectacles. At best I emerge from my experiences, a positive thinker. Perhaps, due to my northern upbringing, I like to call a spade a spade. I prefer to adopt a direct line of approach. Some abhor this kind of frankness. I believe life is too short to observe preliminary etiquette. However, much to my advantage, I quickly discovered that in business, it is necessary to exercise extreme caution. How else can one shed the sheep from among the goats?

Big businessmen have the reputation of being ruthless, of riding rough-shod over their contemporaries. This is not a way of life I should care to be part of. I like to compare running a business to handling a sheep dog: one must be at least 10 jumps ahead. Some people relish living constantly on their wits, whereas I get satisfaction battling against the sheep, the terrain and the elements.

We quickly realised that the purchase of a property is nowhere near the final goal. Locations designated for tourism must be developed in order to provide the necessary facilities — amenities such as ample parking space, toilets, a craft-area and tearoom among others.

If capital is limited it is vital to arrange one's priorities in order of merit. Initially, planning permission must be obtained and plans drawn up by a qualified draughtsman. One hears stories of difficulties in some areas. We cannot speak highly enough about the understanding shown in respect of the urgency of our project by Borders Regional Council.

Except when visitors are elderly or infirm, we planned to start our programme at the farm entrance, where a coach parking area would be constructed. From this point, visitors can proceed to the school where a photograph collection will portray shepherds and their dogs both past and present.

Below the school, the ground will be landscaped, incorporating a loch fed from the burn and a small island. Waterfalls, footpaths and bridges will eventually be created.

If I close my eyes and allow my imagination to run riot, I can visualise what it will look like in years to come — the loch surrounded by graceful willows, their leafy fronds trailing its glassy surface. Velvet bulrushes intermingle with tall iris. Lilies bob as the wind ripples the water and the tiny island, planted with flowering shrubs, presents a mass of colour. To the left of the farm lane a round sheep stell built from stone is planned, where ewes and lambs of popular hill-breeds will be displayed. Beside the steading a huge Dutch barn will provide a spacious shearing area.

The old cottage and buildings, when renovated will make an olde worlde tearoom and craft area. Fortunately the original cooking range is still intact, complete with swee. The upstairs can be used as B&B accommodation.

The sheep dog handling demonstrations will be held in a natural amphitheatre, stretching down the valley, sandwi-ched between the river Tweed and the A701 Moffat to Edinburgh road. To keep the spectators dry in inclement weather a grandstand will eventually be erected.

New kennelling for the dogs is a must, as well as a nursery area where children can play with the puppies.

I believe that true professionalism, like an eye for stock, ia a gift one is born with. It is essential that 'the goods' be produced in both a practical and professional manner, in order that business comes to you and not the other way around.

It is very tempting to advertise in every publication on offer. Here, as in other areas, caution must be exercised. I once was witness to a poor yearling ewe covered from head to tail in horse-flies. She stood quite still, perfectly resigned to her fate — by that time too weak to rid herself of the affliction.

We have found word of mouth to be one of the best forms of advertising.

In business one is weighed down by monumental responsibilities, not only to oneself but also to others. As shepherds we were anchored by our duty to the sheep entrusted in our care, fully in sympathy with the hardship and deprivation of the life.

The responsibilities to others I refer to are, beside one's immediate family, an ever growing group of dependents. These include other business ventures which rely totally on the success of the 'mother' business. From day one there was no shortage of consultants — or business advisers, knocking at the door. They arrived one after another in quick succession.

Apart from the fact that we could not afford to pay them, after coming this far we relished the chance of managing the centre ourselves. All that we really required was someone who could set things out in a professional manner and was good with figures.

It was vital that our venture did not lose its character by

becoming too commercial. We had to be careful not to break away from the original idea. Profit, when available, had to be ploughed back into the land in order to create a model farm.

If I could be granted a wish it would be that every family be given a plot of ground — no matter how small — whether they desire to plant roses, keep pigs, or merely to grow weeds. The ownership of land creates a feeling of security and a sense of responsibility sadly lacking in today's generation. All children should experience the wonderment of viewing the miracle of nature firsthand.

At Tweedhopefoot our predecessors, Mr and Mrs Sharpe, planted no fewer than 70 different species of cultivated shrubs and flowers along the driveway, all of which flourish consecutively, providing a mass of colour all summer long. Quite an accomplishment at 1100ft. The surrounding meadows furnish a delightful background, the land never having experienced the scourge of herbicides or the ravages of the plough. As a result, from the turn of the year until the latter part of October, gentle snowdrop, primrose, bluebell, harebell, marsh marigold, shy violet, orchid, purple and yellow pansy, cuckoo flower, ragged-robin, wild mountain thyme and purple heather, to name but a few, gladden the eye.

Surely, there can be no sweeter aspect, than to awaken with the season's perfume as we do and gaze on such a vast expanse of loveliness, framed by an arbour of sweet-scented honeysuckle.

Owning a farm with no livestock can only be compared with owning a pub with no beer. In the spring of the year Biggar mart kindly credited us with a lively flock of blackfaced hoggs — the balance to be paid when they were sold.

We spent many hours designing a sign for the roadside. Eventually it was finished. Geoff painted a collie dog on either side, the wording read 'Border Collie and Shepherd Centre'.

One morning the telephone rang — on the other end a lady inquired, 'Are they German Shepherds?' She was obviously referring to the canine variety. 'No,' I replied, 'they are British.' It was not until I replaced the receiver that I realised what I had said. Bearing in mind that some overseas visitors have never heard of a Border collie, never mind seen one in action, we decided to alter the name of the establishment to 'Tweedhope Sheep Dogs' thus incorporating the prefix I use for my own collies.

A leaflet was designed and several thousand copies distributed throughout the area. Newspapers, magazines, radio and television networks were informed. Friends all over the globe were told of our intention to open our gates to the public.

In what seemed like no time at all, planning permission was agreed and a grant to improve the existing facilities was applied for through the Scottish Tourist Board. Our heads buzzed with business plans, cashflow forecasts and estimates from plant-hire contractors, fencers, builders and plumbers. 'Grant applications should carry a health warning,' I moaned. Time was of the essence. Ready or not, we had to open in April. The interest on the money we had already borrowed had to be found. I realise now just how a diminutive wren feels nurturing a giant cuckoo.

At last all of the paperwork was completed and the Tourist Board appeared not only satisfied but, more important, enthusiastic. The bombshell fell when our bank was invited to match their grant. Head office considered

*An arbor
of sweet-scented
honeysuckle*

that a further loan at this time might prove too onerous. To say that we felt devastated by the news following all our efforts, is putting it mildly. The decision meant that we would lose a large investment in our property.

There were two options left open to us. We could either sit and feel sorry for ourselves, or we could open regardless. Naturally we chose the latter, relying solely on the pull of our four-legged friends.

We took stock of our assets. In our opinion the scenery was unbeatable. Two litters of puppies were due, and the 'wee school' would make an ideal craft shop for the time being. We at once got busy with paint brushes and decorated the building dark green with a cheerful red roof. Several old desks, complete with graffiti, were obtained from Peebles High School and an easel was purchased from a nearby dealer in antiques. Hundreds of photographs were carefully labelled and mounted on large sheets of card. These we riveted to the wooden walls of the newly-whitened classroom.

A celebrity corner boasted autographed documentation of, believe it or not, young Geoff's heroes, the A Team, my idol, the film star Randolph Scott, and television broadcasters Barry Norman and the late Ray Moore.

A welcome recruit arrived, in the shape of Carol, from nearby Stobo — along with her spinning wheel. She filled the little school with masses of pretty flowers and various home-made crafts. We had met the previous spring when she purchased a puppy with which to shepherd her small flock of Shetland ewes.

A dear friend of many years standing who paid us an early visit was Bobby Mitchell. Bobby possesses a gentle charm that is immediately obvious to all who make his acquaintance, plus an inveterate appetite for knowledge of

'Two litters of puppies were due'

the rural scene. He has dedicated his entire life to both the Clydesdale horse and the Border collie. His first recollection of the former was around the year 1920, when his father and grandfather owned a coach hire business in the Peeblesshire village of Romanno Bridge. His pride and joy is a unique collection of photographs depicting 'these great animals' — Bobby's own description of them — going back to the beginning of the Clydesdale stud books. Among them are some early likenesses sketched before cameras were invented. The whole collection covers a period of almost 70 years.

Regarding sheep dogs, Bobby has in his possession a store of data covering a period of at least 200 years. His Border collie pedigrees spanning five generations, drawn in a large circle with the names and registration numbers of the first generation appearing in the centre, are prepared with obvious artistic skill and neatness. A helpful feature is that the particulars of the male line are written in blue, while the female line is in pink.

Bobby's other hobbies are stick dressing and carpentry. One of the nicest house-warming gifts we received was a wooden bird table depicting a white-faced ewe and a collie dog. It was made by Bobby after Tarka our horse tried to remove a crust of bread from the previous table, demolishing it completely.

Bobby admitted that he was more than delighted to visit 'Up Tweed', as the saying goes. His connection with the area was through his grandfather who in his younger days was manager at Stanhope, where the shepherd poet John Dixon herded.

When I was a young child living in a town I harboured secret ambitions like many children of that time. For

The classroom in the Wee School

instance, I longed to be able to hold a baby lamb, to sit astride a pony, preferably my own, or simply to spend time playing with a litter of cuddly puppies.

All of these and more we hope to be able to provide for the enjoyment of visiting youngsters.

When first we opened our doors to the public I admit to experiencing some feelings of trepidation about the interests of today's children. For example, the entertainment on offer at the present time through the media of television, exhibits a distinct scientific flavour.

As it happened my doubts were unfounded. The enraptured gazes accompanied by childish giggles, heard when observing the antics of lambs, puppies, kittens and even the odd duckling that chose to appear, quickly dispelled any misgivings. One instance in particular stands out in my mind. The father of a small, fair-haired Dutch boy actually got into his car and drove out of the yard leaving him behind because the child refused to be parted from a litter of puppies. He stopped on reaching the main road and was treated to the sight of his young son, a pup tucked under one arm, waving goodbye to him. Added to this, the look of rapture on the face of a blind, physically handicapped girl, when I placed a new-born pup in her outstretched hands, will stay with me always. It is everyday experiences such as these that make it all worthwhile.

From the point of view of adult visitors, I decided that in order of priority a warm welcome would come high on the list, followed by value-for-money entertainment in beautiful surroundings and finally, they should be able to discuss what they had heard and seen over a cup of tea before choosing a tasteful memento to remind them of their day. Goods in the craft shop include my husband's crooks, prints, stationery, my books, knitwear and numerous other

Carol at the spinning wheel

items manufactured by country folk.

It was not until the following season, when the place began to take on a more business-like air that salesmen selling various trinkets began to call. It would have been easy at this time to break away from the original shepherding theme, had we not been determined to sustain it. Besides the sheep dog handling demonstrations that were given seven days a week during the first season, morning coffee and afternoon teas were provided on the lawn in front of the house. Bed and breakfast accommodation was also on offer.

Young sheep dogs belonging to farmers, providing they were fully vaccinated, were taken in for training. Six weeks was needed to get them useful close at hand.

Throughout the summer representatives from the Borders Regional Council Community Programme, the Countryside Commission for Scotland and the Scottish Tourist Board made regular visits to Tweedhopefoot in order to observe how we were progressing.

In all, around 2000 visitors passed through our gates that first season, among them John Roberts, the American vice-president of the Busch Entertainment Corporation and his family, who were holidaying in Scotland. John's company provides entertainment annually for six million holidaymakers. He kindly wrote glowing testimonials on our behalf, to all the aforementioned.

A second business plan and forecast was painstakingly prepared for the bank's head office. Estimates were again obtained, all to no avail. Surety in the shape of £12,000 was requested before further financial help was forthcoming.

Because the provision of surety was the only option, we accepted, against our principles, a much appreciated offer from a private source.

Bobby Mitchell and Carnation

Out of the profit we made during our first season we were given permission by the bank to purchase a flock of ewes. We chose blackfaced drafts, some of which had seen better days. At £25 a head they were a gift, especially as we discovered a number of young sheep among them. When we left Bowmont we brought along with us four south country Cheviot sheep. These included a couple of wethers, named Tweedledee and Tweedledum, a gimmer called Charlotte and a ram lamb, who answered when he felt inclined, to the name of Charlie. The quartet had lived in our garden, acting as lawnmowers. Charlie had been kept originally for breeding but unfortunately he had turned out slightly 'shuttle-gobbed' or 'sow-mouthed', as the affliction is sometimes described.

After a few months 'Up Tweed', to our relief Charlie's lower jaw quickly grew to match his upper — perhaps because he was no longer required to act as a lawnmower. Unfortunately he will never make 'a good un', being short and round in stature, instead of the stipulated long and square.

Through being handled regularly in the demonstrations he has developed into quite a character. In fact he could be described as our main asset. There came an occasion when a small child was lifted on to his back. Charlie took the event in his stride; splaying his short sturdy legs for added support he regurgitated extravagantly and continued chewing with what can only be described as a contented expression on his knobbly face. These 'rides' are now a regular feature with the smaller visitors and Charlie has become the most photographed Cheviot in Britain.

The birdtable

ENGLEBERT AND HUMPERDINK

Lustrous red berries clothed in a white hoar frost, accompanied by early morning mist, followed by a lazy warm sun: it was a belated Indian summer that missed by a whisker an all too brief opportunity to enhance the fiery bent, the falling leaves and the changing spruce. All had died to mellow gold. November has arrived, the beginning of the sheep year as far as upland flockmasters are concerned. This day we took delivery of Humperdink, an enormous blue-headed Leicester shearling ram who arrived complete with an understudy whom we named Englebert. The latter was on loan to 'chase-up' once the rush is over and most of our blackies had been put in-lamb by his superior partner. On arrival, 'the boys' were gently persuaded into the hilly field at the far-side of the property, where Charlie the demonstration ram speedily introduced himself, by delivering a smart broadside into poor Englebert's ribs. We were quick to separate them. Small rams such as Charlie have an unpleasant habit of breaking the necks of larger ones with a powerful butt to the nose end.

We bought Humperdink in early October. His owner kindly offered to keep him until the time was ripe.

Geoff was judging Manor Sheep Dog Trial, one of the more scenic events on our calendar. Laddie and I had competed unsuccessfully. My young bitch, Holly, at this her second trial, had pleased me greatly by her efforts but unfortunately had failed to pen.

Once the prizegiving was over we made the acquaintance of a curly-haired young man who introduced himself as Iain Campbell of Glenrath. After talking for only a few moments it became obvious that here was someone totally dedicated to his extensive rugged domain and the sheep

Charlie...is our darling

stock that grazed there.

Geoff and I were at this time seeking a ram of the blue-headed variety to cross with our ewes, in the hope of producing a quantity of female mule lambs, much favoured by lowland farmers for the production of fat lambs.

All flockmasters know that the ram is half the flock. Our flock consisted of 114 fairly fit ewes and at that time we could not afford a ram of show proportions. However, no matter how modest our purse it was important to invest in one, preferably bred on high ground, physically fit and one of twins.

Iain had rams to sell — twin shearlings. 'They were triplets, but one died at birth', he added. 'Both are proven breeders, we used them last year as lambs.' Would we care to follow him and take a look?

Both us and the dogs hurriedly piled into the car and after driving a short distance along the haugh, overshadowed by steep autumn tinted hills, we finally ground to a halt at the burnside. The far bank was sown down to a succulent crop of rape, itself an enterprising achievement in such testing terrain. An even flock of this year's lambs nibbled greedily at the luscious leaves, standing belly deep in the dew soaked foliage; the stench of their steamy breaths cutting the evening air like a knife. They bleated suspiciously to one another as we splashed across the water, and after craning their necks in order to snatch a last bite, turned lazily away at the sight of my dog.

I cautiously sent Laddie around the perimeter at Iain's bidding. The two rams were standing snootily by themselves and were therefore easily shed in our direction. Geoff passed an experienced eye over their qualifications. One was slightly better in his conformation than his rangier brother. However, their owner informed us that the latter

Laddie

was the better breeder regarding type, having more crimp in his fleece, an important attribute that he passed on to his daughters. He was also more blue about the face and ears as well as being finer boned, essential for milkiness in the resulting progeny. Theoretically the more blue or black the sire, the better the chance of producing the more popular dark-faced ewe. Believe me, sheep fashion is equally comparable to human whims.

Finally, after a serious debate on crimp in wool, during which I asked our host how his own hair became so curly, it was time to go home. We re-crossed the burn, this time through deep water and while I paused to empty my soaking wellies, Geoff suggested to Iain that we sleep on it and let him have our decision regarding which ram, the following day. However, before we had gone a couple of miles along the road we had made our choice. The ram with the crimped hairstyle would do nicely. His name would be Humperdink, which was perhaps wishful thinking on our part.

If only winter days could be fashioned from elastic —
rather that they should stretch instead of shrink.
If only we could be born old and grow young ...

A wintry sun rode high in a near cloudless blue sky as startled sheep scattered down the valley. Slender translucent fingers of ice adorned the ragged edges of the Tweed. Winter flattened reeds crackled underfoot as the dogs, happy to be alive, posed, crept, flanked and raced ahead of me.

In the distance, Tweedhopefoot chimney reeked grey woodsmoke, spiralling vertically, assuring fine weather.

On this chill Thursday, almost 12 months to the day

The old cottage, before and after

following our arrival, we were given the go-ahead from the bank to begin developing the business known as 'Tweedhope Sheep Dogs,' as a centre for tourism.

As soon as the festive season was over, transformation was begun in earnest with the help of grant assistance from The Countryside Commission. Fortunately, the weather was as dry as a bone when the heavy plant moved in and due to the extremely low temperatures, the ground was iron-hard ensuring no scarring whatsoever.

An extremely efficient team of three men using a crane, a bulldozer and a dump truck quickly transformed the uneven area beyond the old cottage into a spacious parking area. The road leading into the farm was raised and widened in order to make it more accessible and a small loch was excavated below the school. Weeping willow, iris and bulrush were donated by Strathclyde Regional Council. Twelve hundred broad-leaved trees were purchased and planted in and around the entrance to the farm by boys on a Youth Training Scheme. Steps were made leading to the school and new fences were erected. A stone wall which separated the demonstration area was demolished and transported to where we planned to build a stell.

An extremely generous grant from the Scottish Tourist Board made the renovation of the old cottage, plus fixtures and fittings, possible. Toilet facilities were provided with help from the Countryside Commission. Jim Bane, a stockman turned artist — nicknamed by me 'Precious Bane' — painted several imposing roadside signs depicting a crouching collie. At a later date, his sons decorated the entire establishment both inside and out in black and white — true sheep dog colours.

In January, 1988, I rose up in the world with the purchase of a word processor at a little over the cost of a

Tweedhopefoot steading

Top: *Alberta Open Sheep Dog Trial.* Bottom: *The rough and the smooth — from left, Glen, Holly, Sir Garry and Laddie*

*With
Lord Sanderson
Minister of
Agriculture
for Scotland*

new typewriter. This buy helped make the task of writing and the preparation of business documents less time-consuming.

We had made provisions to have the entrance to the driveway widened so as to admit coaches from both directions. The previous summer vehicles pausing at the roadside in order to observe the dogs had been causing a road hazard. So much so that the council decided that, in the interest of road safety, they would provide a lay-by with the help of a 60% grant from the Countryside Commission.

Work began in March when we experienced some of the coldest winter weather. Watching from the warmth of the kitchen, I felt a great deal of sympathy for the council workers who were having to labour in such an exposed area. As the work progressed we were treated daily to the exciting roar and rumble of accelerating bulldozers, the cautionary high pitched bleep of reversing trucks, the toot of horns and the whoosh of air-brakes. Orange warning lights flashed on and off as workmen toiled relentlessly in the bitter north-east wind. Never was so much accomplished by so few in such a short space of time.

The month of March also saw the arrival of 18 tons of pebbles to be spread in the yard, and our very first lamb, born on the banks of the Tweed out of Charlotte, sired by Cheviot Charlie.

Our visitor season began in April in the midst of lambing time. During the six months that followed 3000 people flocked through our gates to attend demonstrations and sheep dog trials. Life was hectic to say the least. Nevertheless, we decided to take Saturdays off in order to keep our hand in at local trials.

In July, along with the dogs we were presented to Her

Majesty the Queen and His Royal Highness the Duke of Edinburgh at Broughton School during their visit to Tweeddale, Her Majesty, looking from Laddie to Holly asked if there was any difference between the rough-coated and the smooth. To my great delight, old Garry received a royal pat on the head and since that day has been dubbed Sir Garry by all.

Immediately after our royal encounter we rushed to Edinburgh Airport to catch a flight to Canada, leaving the dogs, sheep and young Geoff in the capable hands of my sister-in law, Anne, her husband, Dick, and their children. Nine hours later, we touched down in Calgary, Alberta, land of cracked windscreens, piranha mosquitoes and genuine cowboys. We had been invited by Richard and Mary Lynne Tipton to judge three sheep dog trials and give a training seminar. The Tiptons and their artistically talented son live in an authentic log cabin they built themselves overlooking a beaver lodge. The fun and hospitality experienced there has yet to be equalled by us. At the end of 11 informative days and nights we returned to Tweedhopefoot in time to meet Lord Sanderson of Bowden, the Scottish Minister of Agriculture, who paid us a visit in order to examine our methods of farm diversification.

Throughout the spring and summer months we were provided with much appreciated help from Lynette Millville, an American on a working holiday, and Tommy, Hilary and Dorothy, who contributed enormously in making our efforts a success.

4
HOLLY

THE GREYHOUND

Headed lyke a snake,
Neckyed lyke a drake,
Fotyd lyke a cat,
Tayled lyke a ratte,
Syded lyke a teme,
And cheyned lyke a bream.

This thirteenth-century poem scribed by Wynkyn de Werde aptly describes Trim's great granddaughter, my beautiful bitch Holly. Her disposition is as sweet as the purest heather honey and her gentle liquid brown eyes constantly seek mine for approval. Her black and white markings are hand-painted and her gleaming skin mirrored like a seal. Her slender agile limbs scarcely touch the ground as she effortlessly skims the dyke backs.

Born at Holly Bush Farm at Christmas, 1985, in the vicinity of Abbotsford, home of Sir Walter Scott, Holly's sire is Simon Clarke's big bare-skinned Roy. She was part of a litter of six lively puppies whose ever watchful dam Nan is the daughter of an earlier Holly that we bred out of Trim several years ago.

It was a clear, crisp, starlit evening when we set forth by car to view Nan's puppies. What I remember most about the outing was my feet flying from under me on a patch of ice in Simon's yard and finding myself lying flat on my

Holly, above, and Jill — alias 'Miss America'

back in a most undignified pose. Worse than that, I had been the one entrusted with Nan's supper.

Simon's charges were all 'well done' as we say, meaning, in good fettle. Even in these so-called enlightened times one witnesses litters of undernourished, worm infested pups. These were lively, bright of eye and cleanly bedded. which says a lot for a young shepherd living in a bachelor pad, caring for hundreds of sheep.

Holly caught my attention from the moment I entered the building. She was very like Jan, 'the Bionic Bitch' that my husband had owned a few years previously. A shepherd once wrote 'pick a pup that speaks to you'. So I did, and was delighted to learn that just as soon as she was weaned from her mother Simon would bring her over. She had been overlooked by other buyers due to her greyhound appearance. It had been remarked that she resembled a rat rather than a Border collie.

Until I made the acquaintance of Holly, I must admit to not being over-enamoured by the 'slape-haired' variety, as they are sometimes described south of Northumberland. Holly very quickly became the exception to the rule, completely winning me over with her streamlined appearance, super intelligence, character and classical method of working. Other major advantages being that smooth-coated dogs are much easier to keep clean and do not ball up with snow in wintry weather.

I used to like to see all livestock, whether it be male or female strongly made and thick set, with heavy bone. Now I realise that there are 'horses for courses'. A fine-boned female is often prolific and 'milky' whereas a heavy one is not. The breeding of a powerful masculine type of male from a feminine type female, as any good Blackface or Cheviot breeder will tell you, is to be recommended.

Holly proved to be an extrovert right from the word go. Her particular kind of mannerisms as yet undetected in any of our other dogs. For instance, after consuming her evening meal she will expertly tilt her dish onto its side holding it in position with her paw, whilst she licks the outer rim. When it comes to escapology she knows no equal. We nick-named her Houdini and have yet to discover a door she cannot open either by sheer force or ingenuity. Recently she was left alone for a few minutes in the kitchen. On my return I was surprised to find three sliding doors, plus the refrigerator, standing agape.

In early June, 1987, Holly was heavy in pup to my husband's dog Cap; a prick-eared, bare-skinned, carefully bred dog, going back to Les Morrison of Cleugh Brae's Sweep and Midge, Johnny Rogerson's Laddie and the late John Gilchrist's Spot. All of whom were outstanding trial dogs and good breeders. In his misguided youth, mischievous Cap had the endearing habit of playfully nipping my nether regions.

Young Geoff is Cap's greatest fan. He named him 'Bruno' after his favourite British heavyweight boxer. Of Cap he says, 'He's a lean, mean, fighting machine.'

Without a doubt, young Geoff's loyalty lies with his dad's dogs. He calls them The A Team, whilst mine go under the unflattering title of The Gay Team.

At the same time as Holly's pregnancy, Lucy, her kennel mate was also carrying a litter. On the second day of June, before we had barely finished lunch, Lucy went into labour, quickly producing two large dog puppies without any fuss or bother. She pupped in comfort on a redundant couch in the byre. Her sons were resplendent in black satin waistcoats with snowy white collars and cuffs. By evening poor Holly's envy knew no bounds. She decided on a spot

of pup-napping while Lucy was taking a walk, surrepti-
tiously removing the puppies to her own bed in the far
corner where she immediately began suckling them wearing
what can only be described as a smug expression. On her
return, Lucy flopped down completely unconcerned and
proceeded to top and tail her shared offspring.

By June 5th Holly had given birth to her own family of
six healthy puppies — three dogs and three bitches.
Because of a shortage of room both litters were housed in
the same building. Holly insisted that all the puppies shared
the same nest, namely her own, and resisted any effort to
part them. Lucy quickly tired of motherhood while Holly
revelled in it.

Holly reminded me of a little girl at school we all looked
on as 'mother' because of her caring attitude. Her strong
maternal instinct is very much in evidence in her work.
When she gathers our sheep together it is done without
hassle or disturbance to her charges. She quietly floats
around on the distant horizon tidying the other young dogs'
mistakes, fetching the sheep that they leave and flushing out
any hidden stragglers.

Like all 'guid' beasts I cannot recall giving her any
training, she just sort of happened, everything slipping into
place on its own — a most natural animal. Her example
only convinces me further that good dogs, like good people,
are born and not made.

Throughout the summer months, from a tender age, she
performed tirelessly alongside my other two dogs, learning
both sets of commands as well as amusing the visitors with
her total independence.

Neal Fadler, a sheep dog handler, trainer and Gary
Cooper lookalike — 'only taller,' he hastened to add —
travelled from Washington State, across America and over

Holly with Jill, left, and Glen

the Atlantic Ocean to take delivery of Jill, alias Miss America, one of Holly's offspring. She, Miss A, was the runt of the litter and by the time of her departure she had completely won my heart. I would have given anything to keep her because she exhibited many of her mother's amusing traits. Until Jill had finished eating none of the rest of the litter dared to as much as sniff at their food. They would all sit patiently in a row until she became replete. Whenever I entered their living quarters the wee moron drove her companions smartly away, jealously nipping their flanks before returning to reap all the attention.

On his return to America Neal wrote of her: 'She was a real little trooper all the way home, never flagging or complaining on the long flight.' Then came an almost poetic description that not only gladdened my heart but also made me feel justifiably proud of both man and dog. 'I am constantly amazed,' Neal wrote, 'by the instinct that little Jill shows on sheep. She has an authority that is pure pleasure to see in action. She still doesn't have any working commands on her but I put her to sheep twice a week to just let her work things out and develop her sheep sense. She is growing at a good rate and is sound in every way. I can shush her out and around and by positioning myself rightly get her to fetch evenly. She runs naturally to the left but she is now beginning to go right with just a little urging and is widening out in the process. Her manner doesn't upset sheep, yet when she moves in sheep move for her in an even positive way. She shows a good amount of eye and has a smooth soft touch unless somebody challenges her. She can be as soft as velvet or as hard as stone depending upon the situation facing her. Even one old Suffolk ewe that sometimes likes to fight with some of the other dogs doesn't put up much resistance before she turns back in with the rest of the sheep and moves on. Besides all of her great intensity and desire to work she shows a wonderful personality which is always a source of fun for us. She is of course very curious and observant about anything that goes on around her. So we never tire of her antics.'

All of Holly's litter were found good, working homes. Only Glen, a strongly made perfectly marked black and white dog pup remained. He is pleasing me immensely and proving to be as classy as his mother, in a 'doggy' sort of way. Apart from his low slung tail he reminds me of a pointer with a dash, and only a dash mind you, of greyhound and mastiff blood.

In young Glen we are looking for a 'super stud'. Only time will tell if he is of that worthy calibre. When he was only seven weeks old he greatly impressed me by cocking his leg at a fence post. Admittedly he lost his balance and almost tumbled over but at least he made the attempt, which must put him in with a chance.

5

GARRY —
OLD MAN
OF THE HILLS

My devoted dog Garry is now in his fifteenth year. A dear old gentleman with a luxurious curly coat who still manages the odd stint around the sheep, often putting the younger dogs to shame with his clever workmanship and steady intelligent method. His soft brown eyes, though glazed by cataracts, show great enthusiasm for the work though he knows his limitations. He rarely takes a command and one would therefore assume that his hearing is impaired. Not so, I only need ask if he would like some dinner and he immediately licks his lips and wags his tail.

He is still without a doubt the most well-mannered dog that I have ever come across. When his dish is placed before him, no matter how hungry, he will always raise his head in order to 'speak' his thanks, a reaction that his son, Laddie, has also adopted. Garry has never in his life stolen food from the table, though meat has often been left upon it.

He has become a veritable chatterbox in his old age and speaks both to us and anyone else who cares to listen, using gentle grunts and sighs. If possible, age has made him even more endearing.

Throughout the summer months, so as not to be outdone, he insisted on joining in the sheep dog demonstrations,

Garry — old man of the hills

endeavouring to steal the limelight away from Laddie and Holly. Unfortunately, Holly, being younger, worked in a higher gear than the old dog and things did not always turn out as planned.

Garry insisted on doing his own thing and caused great amusement to the onlookers by only running halfway up the field on his outrun, leaving the other two to perform the leg-work, thus saving his energy for the grand finale.

A favourite memory that for me will always hold pride of place regarding Garry's wisdom occurred when he was all of two years old. Gail Dapogny, an American, was staying with us at the time. We were standing below the house admiring the wonderful view of Cheviot and the surrounding hills when I put Garry away to gather the south face of Swindon, the summit being some two miles away.

In his youth he was marvellous at putting different cuts of sheep together without being given any commands to guide him. Often he was to be seen crouching motionless in a favourable position, allowing the sheep to do the running.

Eventually the whole face was gathered together and Garry proceeded steadily downhill with his charges, keeping a nice distance so that the sheep automatically moved before him no matter how large the flock, with only his strength of eye, coupled with great determination, holding them to him as though attached by a piece of elastic.

There were two large fields to pass through before Garry reached us with the flock. This meant him cross-driving for several hundred yards and negotiating two gateways. The gate into the first field was standing wide open and the sheep passed through without any problems. The hurdle into the second field, unknown to me, had been tied up with string. Garry patiently flanked back and forth trying, to no avail, to drive his charges through. Remembering another gap halfway up the fence in the opposite direction, I was tempted to whistle Garry into the corner. However, before my fingers reached my mouth Garry swung in on his own, expertly driving the flock uphill until the gap was reached. All of this small drama took place on the other side of Bowmont Water, at least half a mile away. I remember feeling very humble on that particular occasion, an emotion that I have experienced on many occasions since. No words were spoken, none were needed. When finally I glanced across at my companion I noticed that there were tears of admiration glistening in her eyes.

A TRIBUTE TO GARRY

True friends are hard to find and keep,
When the ground is rough and the hill is steep,
On the Cheviot brae we herded sheep
Me and my old friend Garry.
The bonny pup that first I saw,
Became a dog abune them a',
His back like jet, his breist like sna',
My handsome, faithful, Garry.

My lifetime partner he has been,
And many's the gatherin' we hae seen,
There' no a dog wa worked sae keen,
As my trusty old friend Garry.
O'er hills and glens we strode the heather,
Worked as a team in any weather,
We faced the trials o' life thegither,
Me and my old friend, Garry.

My every thought is his command,
'Away tae me', 'come bye' and 'stand'.
The finest collie in the land,
That's my trusty Garry.
But his soft brown eyes have lost their glow,
His flying legs are getting slow,
And the time will come when he must go,
My trusty old friend, Garry.

Dogs like my Garry are so few,
And when his time on earth is through,
I'll whisper one last 'that'll do',
To my trusty old friend, Garry.
But his memory will never dim,
My thoughts will always be with him,
And he'll lie at peace like Jed and Trim,
Fareweel my faithful Garry.

S. Gray

A FEW DAYS IN THE BORDERS
by Gail Dapogny

A sheep dog trial followed by three days accompanying a
shepherd and his dogs in their day to day work in the
Border region of Scotland... Never would I have imagined
that my short visit to Europe this past June could end with
such an experience, but it did just that.

We were in Denmark because of my husband's
engagements there as a jazz pianist, and it had been a
delightful visit; but the tantalising thought of Scotland only
1000 miles away was on my mind constantly. The prospect
of travelling alone across Europe to get there intimidated

me considerably, but in the end the temptation was more than I could withstand. Thirty six hours, three trains and a long boat trip later, I found myself pulling into the beautiful city of Edinburgh, past the dramatic cliffs that mark its outskirts. This was a Sunday morning, and I was by then travel weary and confused. Somehow the conviction that I would find Border collies if I could just get to Scotland had overruled all common sense; now that I was here, standing alone with a mound of luggage on a busy street in a huge city, the trip seemed like madness.

A tourist bureau caught my eye, and I trudged down a long hill to investigate. Dozens of posters advertised exciting sounding tours, but I had eyes for one thing only… what I had most hoped to find, a sign sandwiched down in a corner with that day's date, announcing 'Sheep Dog Trial, Floors Castle, Kelso, Scotland.' After obtaining details, checking luggage and changing clothes, I was on my way again — this time by bus — 50 miles into the Scottish Borders. We drove past miles of stone walls, a characteristic sight in that country. In this case marking the boundaries of a huge estate. The bus driver let me off at the entrance, and I walked half a mile through the rolling grounds of Floors Castle, home of the Duke and Duchess of Roxburghe. I had begun to wonder whether there was indeed a sheep dog trial when I heard a far off whistle and saw the flash of black and white of a Border collie on an outrun. Right then, all fatigue, all foreign country strangeness melted away and I knew I was in the right place!

The trial was an invitation event sponsored by McEwan's lager. There were around 60 competitors, and the programme read like a *Who's Who* of Scottish handlers Gilchrist, Templeton, Bathgate, Richardson (judging), and so on. And the quality lived up to expectations. I was impressed over and over with the superb control and with the type of handling — quiet, gentle, affectionate, The good feeling between dogs and handlers was strongly apparent both on the trial course and off. I alternately watched the engrossing trial and talked with cordial competitors (and of course tried to take in 60 Border collies in one place). Everyone was friendly and considerate; some seemed eager, even, to chat about American dogs and handlers. John Templeton was particularly nice to me, and I was proud to be able to tell him that he was the breeder of my own Border collie's grandfather. It was interesting that many of the questions had to do not so much with trial winners in America as with the quality of dog care and treatment — again, the welfare of the dog seemed an ever-present concern. Classic markings and colouring were predominant in the dogs I saw and, surprisingly to me, many of the handlers showed considerable interest in the appearance of the dogs. The conviction that we all emphatically share that the Border collie should not be recognised for conformation showing did not lessen their pride in all aspects of their dogs fitness, intelligence, temperament and appearance. I also became aware of the conviction — increasingly widespread evidently — on the part of many that, in terms of breeding, good sound dogs are more important than specific and famous lines.

Sometime during the afternoon I struck up a conversation with a husband and wife team, Geoff and Viv Billingham who were both competitors in the trial.

The trial ended in the early evening with a fascinating brace event, and here the team work, three way, was particularly refined, not to mention demanding. Geoff had an especially fine run in brace, although he was characteristically modest about this as he is about his impressive trial record.

The Billinghams invited me to stay with them for a few days, and I gratefully accepted. They live with their son, also Geoff, in a shepherd's cottage (actually an old two storey house) 15 miles further into the hills, near the village of Yetholm. There, on the edge of the Cheviots, Geoff works as a shepherd, tending some 800 ewes, Cheviots and Blackfaces, with his 10 dogs on 1200 hilly acres. The unspoiled beauty of the land is breathtaking, great expanses of hill covered with all those plants one associates with Scotland — moss, gorse, bracken, fern, heather on the tops, and dark forests and higher hills unfolding as far in the distance as one can see. My stay in Scotland was memorable indeed. I was driven around the area and taken by Viv to work her dogs. She tried in vain to teach me to whistle through my fingers. She is one of a small but growing group of lady handlers unmistakably serious and determined.

Geoff, whose talents include stick dressing and elegant pencil drawings is a gentle calm man who paid me the ultimate compliment of allowing me to accompany him on his twice daily treks into the hills, leaving each morning at 5.30 for hours, and going out again in the early evening following tea until 10.30pm or so — perhaps eight hours in all. Those hours were unforgettable ones. We climbed about two miles up each hill; that is, he climbed, easily of course, while I puffed and lurched along behind. (The shepherd's crook is an absolute necessity in that terrain.) Frequently the dogs would drop back to push a friendly muzzle into my hand and grin up at me reassuringly.

Often for reasons of covering the ground, we separated, and once late on in the evening I was able to see not only Geoff and his dogs working but, far in the distance, another shepherd and his dogs driving a flock up a hillside to disappear eventually into the clouds and darkness. Geoff informed me that this operation of teaching the lambs to go up on to the tops at night in order to allow the haughs (valley bottoms) to recover, was practised all over Scotland and in hilly regions elsewhere.

Looking on this panoramic view I had to keep reminding myself that all of this wasn't some vast show staged for my benefit!

The rapport between dog and master takes on a special meaning in hills such as these. There is a fine balance of responsiveness from the dogs to their master and a quite remarkable ability to think for themselves. Often the dogs would disappear for 10 to 15 minutes at a time, emerging finally on some distant hill driving ewes and lambs and sharply scanning the slopes for the one that stayed behind. Such a situation obviously calls for truly sensitive handling, and Geoff seems to possess a remarkable sixth sense with his dogs, knowing precisely when to rely on their judgment. Frequently he pointed out the importance of having sound versatile hill dogs; he had justifiable pride in his team — top trial competitors at the weekends, working with such extraordinary independence and skill in the difficult terrain and unpredictable demands of Scottish hills. I couldn't take my eyes off those dogs, the vitality, the uncanny perceptiveness, devotedness to their master and of course that special Border collie sweetness.

Geoff taught me much. Through his careful explanations I came to see the difference between 'a good worker' and a 'truly special' dog. One of his dogs in particular — a top trial winner — was a joy to watch, floating over the ground with remarkable grace, anticipating the sheeps' movements long before anyone else. The experienced dogs were strong where necessary, but they also were gentle, or in Geoff's words 'good to the sheep'. We watched one little bitch move an entire flock including many tiny lambs down a steep rocky hillside; her control was flawless, never putting on too much pressure. It was interesting to note that these dogs remained standing in their work instead of dropping, a dog either taught to be upstanding or naturally inclined that way is more desirable on rough hill ground. And always the dogs returned to their master for the affectionate pat on the head that followed work well done.

There were plenty of amusing moments, even aside from my huffing and puffing, riding on the back of the tractor in the cold crisp morning air with three affectionate collies crowding on my lap; the sound of the curlew, so similar to Geoff's whistles that occasionally the dogs obeyed a bird signal by mistake, then turned back with a puzzled expression on their faces. My endless ignorant questions: 'What's a moor?' 'You're standing on one.' We kept a constant look-out for the unshorn sheep stranded on their backs and on one occasion we went in search of an exhausted ewe to give her a calcium injection for 'staggers'. It was surprisingly easy to lose one's bearings in that country. The hills appeared sharp and clear from down below, but higher up the glens and burns and rocks and patches of mist and even sometimes low clouds dissolve the clarity. The quiet seemed intense, broken only by the bleating of the sheep and the singing of the larks overhead, An occasional fox popped up for a look as did the odd hare. The dogs gave all of this an indifferent sniff and kept to their business. Now and then we paused on a peak, both caught up in that peculiar stillness that seems to belong to high places.

'Memorable' seems rather an inadequate word as I recall

the first time that I stood on a slope and watched them, an old age-old team, that of a shepherd and his dogs, working together on a distant Scottish hillside, the whistles sounding faintly, the dogs sweeping in endless patterns. A humble and unforgettable experience for a spectator.

Geoff demonstrates hand shearing

6
TWEED —
THE HISTORY OF
THE AREA

Soon after we arrived at Tweedhopefoot Tony Iley, a shepherd author, at present living in the College valley, sent me the following:

DIARY OF A SHEPHERD
July, 1971

'It was the practice in the district for shepherds to help one another at busy times. Walter Fleming of Howclough was on with his hay that day and so he asked me to take his place at the Tweedhopefoot clipping.

Alan Crozier of The March, Elvanfoot, came round to Harthope for me around 10am and we were soon at Tweedhopefoot. When we arrived five 'herds were busy shearing on the wool sheets spread on the ground. Jack Hogarth's father was catching and doing some wool wrapping. Eventually, Jack Hogarth of Tweedhopefoot arrived with another cut of sheep and put them in the pens with Moss, a mainly black dog by T.T. McKnight's late Jaff, out of a bitch got by Alan Gordon's Tweed. Jack then began catching and his father wrapping wool as we six sheared. Jack's young son who was about 11 or 12 ran around doing various jobs. After we had sheared 50 or 60 ewes a halt was called, shears sharpened and we drank a

Girls pack the wool during the shearing

bottle of beer. We began to shear again and managed another 60 before dinner, then we had a second beer before making our way across the shaky bridge that spanned the Tweed, to Jack's cottage and steading.

Jack commented that it would likely be the last shearing time at Tweedhopefoot. We fell into smothered conversation about forestry, knowing that Jack's sheep were going off at the back end of the year to make way for trees. We then went up to the house and after managing to get the tractor and trailer stuck in the burn we had our tea at around six or half past. Afterwards the 'herds dispersed leaving Jack and me to look at the tup lambs.

He was to get the holding of Tweedhopefoot and had already around 60 sheep of his own, mainly bought from The March, Elvanfoot. At the steading Jack showed us two good pups out of Wiston Cap's sister, a bitch of about eight years old. She had made a good job of them. They were by Jack's own dog Moss.'

Surrounding Tweedhopefoot vast armies of spruce mark time on rolling hills where once thousands of sheep peacefully grazed, watched over by generations of shepherds and their faithful collie dogs.

In the month of April the lonely valleys no longer echo with the lyrical bleat of newborn lambs, the anxious baritone of ewes, or the sweet whistled directions of shepherds to their dogs. The curlew's plaintive cry carried on the wind, the mighty thunder of the rushing burn — all are muffled by a never-ending green impermeable blanket.

I hasten to add that, had it not been for the trees, the planting of which greatly reduced the farm's acreage, it is doubtful whether we would ever have been at Tweedhopefoot.

At the time of writing 13% of Scotland is under afforestation. Thirty five thousand acres of Border hill land have been planted, resulting in the loss of home and livelihood to, at the very least, 50 shepherds, their families and the 40,000 breeding sheep in their care.

Over 20% of Dumfries and Galloway is now under trees and in the nearby Ettrick Valley a 15-mile stretch of conifers has been planted.

What price do we place on the eventual loss of precious wildlife? In mid-Argyll, since the 1950s, there has been a 30% decline in the numbers of breeding golden eagles. The Nature Conservancy Council blames the decline on blanket afforestation.

But what of that equally endangered species the hill 'herd, who is willing to champion his cause? Some employers find it more profitable to dispense with a shepherd altogether, to let his home as a holiday cottage and to bring in a student at busy times.

Many shepherds, owing to the insecurity of their existence, are loathe to stand up and be counted. They are by nature a reticent breed, encouraged by their remote life-style to develop natural talents such as painting, drawing, carving in wood and horn, writing poetry and some, having an ear for music, are themselves accomplished musicians.

Personally I do not abhor the planting of conifers. Denuded hillsides look equally boring, whereas thoughtfully planted neat blocks, set out where they will provide shelter belts, can and do enhance an area, especially if mingled with other species. Surely among Scotland's vast acreage there is room for one and all?

During the twelfth and thirteenth centuries the monks that settled at the four main abbeys of Jedburgh, Kelso,

Dryburgh and Melrose brought their weaving skills with them from France and Flanders. They established their flocks in the surrounding hills where they made a large profit exporting wool to the Continent. The first step towards an actual woollen industry came with the invention of the spinning wheel, but it was the demand for mutton during the eighteenth century which made the Borders the textile centre of Britain.

The Blackface sheep with its coarser wool suited to the production of carpets was in some areas replaced by the plump South Country Cheviot which, with its shorter softer fleece, is more suited to the manufacture of finer grades of cloth.

It is interesting to note that in 1896 it was calculated that there were 3000 yarns of thread, 1500 warp and 1500 weft, in a yard of cloth of average weight; so that 'a man in a complete suit of tweed with a tweed overcoat carries around with him more than 20 miles of yarn'.

Hopefully, the economy of the Scottish Borders will depend on the sheep for many years ahead and therefore it is unnecessary to exaggerate the importance of the textile industry to the area.

Already the growing of corn has become less popular in lowland areas; more and more farmers are returning to keeping sheep, with the result that once again there will be employment for shepherds in the lowlands.

(The above information was kindly supplied by the Scottish Tourist Board.)

A cairn at the foot of Hawkshaw Burn is connected with 'a huge and mighty fellow, that robbed all on the way; but was at length, from a mount on the other side of the river, surprised and shot to death'.

JAMES WELSCH
The Babe or Bairn of Tweedhopefoot

At Tweedhopefoot near where Cor Water meets the Tweed there stood an old ale house. From this landmark down to the small village of Tweedsmuir tradition proclaims was the land of giants. For here, in the eighteenth century there dwelt 'a gentle giant' one James Welsch, better known as the 'Bairn' or 'Babe' of Tweedhopefoot. He was an enormous man with an extraordinary physique who, for a wager carried a 20-stone bag of meal across his shoulders from Peebles to his home, a distance of some 25 miles. He was accompanied on the journey by the man who had made the bet, but the pace was so fast that by the time they reached the ford at Drumelzier the fellow was so exhausted that he enquired how he was going to cross the swollen burn. 'Easy settled,' replied the Bairn, 'Jest climb up on tap o' the meal, and I'll carry ye ower.'

Surprised at his offer, and by now totally convinced of the giant's capability, the man from Peebles returned home. The Bairn continued on to Tweedhopefoot, taking only one of the two rests the bargain allowed, thus winning the wager.

It was during the Killing Time that James Welsch and his friend John Hunter, both Covenanters, were pursued by Claverhouse's men. Hunter was shot and killed, while the Bairn managed to escape to his aunt's, who lived in a shepherd's cottage at Carterhope, in the valley of Fruid.

On entering the house the dragoons found a man apparently sleeping by the fire-side. When they began their search the woman rudely awakened him with a clout on the ear, roaring, 'Get up yer lazy lout. Gang oot and haud the sodgers' horses.' His aunt's quick thinking undoubtedly saved his bacon.

John Hunter was killed while fleeing over Erickstane Hill towards the Beeftub. A memorial at that place commemorates the event. He was buried at Tweedsmuir in 1685 and a tombstone erected in 1727 — the only martyr's grave to be found in the Borders.

BONNIE BERTHA OF BADLIEU

In a more romantic vein, there lived around the year 1000AD a beautiful maiden known as 'Bonnie Bertha of Badlieu'. At that time the Scottish King was Kenneth 'the Grim', who was greatly loved by his subjects.

One day while out hunting, Kenneth ventured far from his seat at Polmood into the vast Forest of Caledon. Darkness descended and Kenneth decided to find lodgings for the night. He called at Badlieu and was made welcome by Bertha. It was love at first sight.

Unfortunately Kenneth was already married, but it was a loveless match. He continued to call on Bertha and eventually she bore him a son. Kenneth's wife began to notice his long absences and made it her business to discover his whereabouts.

While he was away fighting the Danes she sent murderers to slay Bertha's household. On his return after victory, Kenneth went first to his court and was surprised to find it in mourning. The queen, they informed him, had been stricken by fever and had died after a short illness.

Making no pretence of his feelings for her, Kenneth at once hastened to Badlieu a free man. When he arrived he found that the hut had been destroyed. Bertha, her father and her baby son were dead and their graves to be found in the peat of the hill-side.

The story goes that Kenneth, broken-hearted, looked to the future. A few years later he led an army against the forces of his cousin Malcolm and met with dire defeat. He was fatally wounded, 'and he who had known love and fatherhood in the lonely Tweed valley, died in anguish'.

TWEED'S WELL

'When a boy, I knew and often still think of a well far up and among the wild hills — alone, without shelter of wall or tree, open to the sun and all the winds. There it lies, ever the same, self-contained, all-sufficient; needing no outward help from stream or shower, but fed from its own unseen unfailing spring. In summer, when all things are faint with the fierce heat, you may see it lying in the dim waste, a daylight star in the blaze of the sun, keeping fresh its circle of young grass and flowers. The small birds know it well and journey from far and near to dip in their slender bills and pipe each his glad song. The sheep dog may be seen halting, in his haste to the uplands, to cool there his curling tongue. In winter, of all waters it alone lives; the keen ice that seals up and silences the brooks and shallows has no power here. Still it cherishes the same grass and flowers with its secret heat, keeping them in perpetual beauty by its soft warm breath.'

Dr John Brown, 1858

THE EDINBURGH MAIL COACH

As early as the year 1715 an ale-house stood at Tweedshaws, which is 1300ft above sea level and close to the source of Tweed.

At one time there existed a number of inns and ale houses on the Edinburgh to Moffat road. After January 1866 many of these places ceased to exist as a result of the abolition of toll bars. It is interesting that clergymen, persons attending their usual places of religious worship, funeral parties, soldiers and volunteers in uniform, as well as horses and carts used in agricultural work, were all exempt from paying toll.

It was at Tweedshaws that an officer in Bonnie Prince Charlie's Highland regiment left behind a silver mounted dirk and sword. One cannot help but wonder what unexpected urgency required that he leave without them.

On the afternoon of February 8, 1831, the Edinburgh mail coach arrived in Moffat from Dumfries in a blinding snowstorm. A new improved road had recently been built at great expense, cutting out the steep hill that ascended the Beeftub via Ericstane Brae. Both Goodfellow, the coach driver, and McGeorge, the guard, were advised not to continue their journey. But fearing that they would lose their jobs insisted on going ahead, taking with them two lady passengers, a couple of men who knew the route and an extra pair of horses.

Three miles from Tweedshaws the horses foundered in deep snow and the coach stuck fast. A pair of horses were unhitched and carried the two men back to Moffat for a chaise with which to rescue the ladies. The driver and guard struggled on with the mail on horseback, however they soon returned after finding the going impossible. McGeorge offered to carry the bags himself, but Goodfellow insisted on accompanying him, such was their dedication to duty.

The two men continued on their way, carrying mail bags weighing seven stones over their shoulders, as the storm increased in fury. Early next morning, when the storm had somewhat abated, the road contractor, a Mr Marchbanks, set out to look for them. After struggling through six miles of deep snow he discovered the mail bags attached to a snow post, bearing blood stains from the frost-bitten fingers that secured them. Enormous snowdrifts made it impossible for Marchbanks to continue, so he returned to Moffat in order to organise a search party. With poles and lanterns they set out to look for the missing men but again failed to discover their whereabouts.

The following day a larger searching party, equipped this time with spades and pick axes, joined in. So difficult were the conditions that it was not until February 12 that the two bodies were discovered near Tweedshaws Cross. (One hundred years after the event, in 1931, a memorial was erected to Goodfellow and McGeorge, close to this spot.)

Apparently, on February 11, 1831, the day before the bodies were found, the Tweedshaws toll keeper visited Dan Kirk, landlord of Tweedshaws Inn, relating a dream he had had in which he saw Goodfellow walking bare-headed with a shepherd on the old road near the cross. Without a moment's hesitation the inn-keeper excitedly described how he had also dreamed of McGeorge in the same place.

Early next morning the two men quietly slipped away from the main body of searchers and arriving at the cross found the two men. Goodfellow was lying stretched on his back and McGeorge on his knees as though in sleep.

MERLIN THE MAGICIAN

When Tweed and Powsail meet at Merlin's grave,
Scotland and England that day ae King shall have.

This prophesy was made by Thomas the Rhymer, the famous thirteenth century seer and poet 'who could tell no lie... '

On the A701 Edinburgh to Moffat road one is suddenly confronted with what can only be described as one of nature's unusual phenomena, a large cavernous hole hundreds of feet in depth, with sides so steep that even agile sheep that graze on the sparse pickings, tread warily. The Devil's Beeftub was once used as a place in which to hide plundered cattle and surely marks the beginning of what must be one of the loveliest and most dramatic valley views in Scotland — Annandale. The name 'Annan' is derived from the Gaelic term for slow running water.

It was here in the land of the pagan Celtic tribe of Selgovae that the Seer Merlin settled after the Battle of Arderydd (Arthuret) fought near Carlisle in 573AD. Dwelling on the slopes of Hartfell, crazed with grief at the slaying of his beloved Gwenddolau, Merlin lived the life of a recluse befriended only by the animals of the forest. It was at this place that he uttered the prophecies which were to influence generations throughout medieval Britain and beyond. According to an early manuscript, Saint Kentigern, Bishop of Glasgow, held conversation with him but the old man had spoken in a foolish manner, foretelling that he would meet a 'three-fold' death. A year later the prophecy

Colvin's fountain at the head of Moffat High Street

was to come true when he was captured by a band of villains who first of all stoned him before casting him down a steep embankment where his battered body became impaled on a salmon stake, before drowning in the Tweed at Drumelzier.

In 1603, on July 25, the day that James VI of Scotland was crowned King of England, a flood altered the course of the Powsail uncovering Merlin's grave.

MOFFAT

Heading south down from the Beeftub past a giant vista of inquisitive peaks, in an area of tranquillity and charm, nestles the small but lively town of Moffat, sometimes called 'The Gateway To Scotland'. The name Moffat is said to come from the Celtic 'magh ubh at' meaning a deep mountain hollow.

With its wide High Street which provides ample parking for both cars and coaches the present day Moffat dates back to the Norman conquest. There is plenty of hotel and B&B accommodation as well as attractive caravan parks, all of which make the town well suited to tourism; most important, the natives, many of whom are in-comers, are both friendly and hospitable.

Geographically Moffat could not be better situated, being at the crossroads of the A74, the Carlisle to Glasgow dual carriageway, and the A701, the Edinburgh to Dumfries route.

Placed as it is, surrounded by dramatic hills and sweeping haughs, the whole area is steeped in history and just waiting to be explored. It is mainly in Moffat that we shop, perhaps once a week and during the wintertime enjoy luncheon at one of the many hotels.

The Balmoral was built in the eighteenth century and was originally known as the Spur Inn. The Black Bull dates back to 1560 and was used as the headquarters for 'Bloody Claverhouse', while The Star Hotel is stated in the record books as being 'the narrowest detached hotel in the UK'.

John, Earl of Hopetoun, nephew to the Marquis of Annandale, was responsible for many of Moffat's major improvements. The southern entrance to the village was widened by demolishing a row of houses. This allowed Lord Kenmure and 1000 supporters to plant the Standard of Mar during the first Jacobite Rebellion in 1715.

John Hopetoun also deepened the churchyard from four to six feet. This unfortunately did away with the older gravestones, but left part of the side-wall of the pre-Reformation kirk, last used in 1790, exposed. A headstone that caught my interest was that of Thomas Weir, shepherd at Green Hill, who met his maker on October 18, 1860. The inscription is as follows:

All ye who come my grave to see,
Prepare my friends to follow me.
Repent in time make no delay.
For I in haste was called away.
Stop now and cast an eye,
As you are now so once were we,
As we are now so must you be.
Short was our lives
Long be our rest.
Christ took us home
When he thought best.

COLVIN'S FOUNTAIN

For me, without any doubt, Colvin's Fountain is the focal point in Moffat. Erected as a gift to the town by William Colvin, of Craigielands, Beattock, in 1875, the architect was Mr Brodie of Edinburgh. The fountain displays as part of its decoration a truly inspiring example of a horned Cheviot ram, resplendent in full fleece.

Since caring for a predominantly Blackface flock, I am really beginning to miss those little Cheviots, especially for training the young dogs. When it comes to pliability and flocking together, they know no equal. Lambing them, of course, is another matter.

On the wall of the Brig Inn, at nearby Beattock, I was treated to the following:

MOODLAW SALES

'For twenty five years from 1851 to 1876 this inn was the place chosen to hold the important Beattock ram sales. Here, about one thousand rams of differing breeds were sold, three-quarters of these, however were Cheviots and the best known and in greatest demand of this breed came from James Brydon's farms at Moodlaw in Eskdalemuir and Kinnelhead, which is three miles up the 'crooked road' above the inn.'

In fact the sales became known as Moodlaw's Sales!

In *Field and Fern* in 1865, H.M. Dixon wrote: 'The old inn hard by the bridge which spans the Evan Water looked quite bright that day with tables spread in the coach house, and as more visitors arrived, table after table was added till at last the coach house threw out skirmishers halfway across the yard.

'Fully 100 shepherd dogs lay about or under the platform and amid the plaided crowd there walked an Edinburgh horse dealer with his hands in his pockets and trying hard to appreciate that cock of the lug and glint of the eye, for which the Moodlaw flock is so famed. All the tups had been collected two or three days before at Mr Brydon's farm Kinnelhead and therefore most of the breeders knew them by heart.'

Yet another version regarding the 'Moodlaw Cheviots' was told by James Scott of Overhall, Hawick, who was better known as the writer and sheep dog handler Troneyhill.

Apparently a 'craze' for improved Cheviot sheep seized flockmasters in the 1860s. It was started by James Bryden who was suspected of having used a Leicester ram to establish his 'improved Cheviots'. He of course strongly denied the accusation.

Brydon's rams sold at an average of £10 at these twice-yearly Beattock sales, a high price in those times. Buyers came from as far afield as America and enormous prices were paid for rams of outstanding conformation. For instance, in 1867, a ram called Craigphadrig was sold for the unheard of price of £194. When it came to good looks Brydon's sheep were indeed superior specimens, with their 'pronounced symmetry'. However, the attraction of these so called improved sheep was short-lived. They did not survive a succession of bad winters as a result of their poor wool and lack of stamina. Mr Brydon eventually went bankrupt and at his dispersal sale, buyers were shocked by the poor condition of his sheep.

The original Cheviots are said to have been brought over by the Spanish Armada. Significant improvements were made to both fleece and conformation when Lincoln blood was introduced by James Robson, of Belford, Bowmont Water, in the mid-eighteenth century.

TWEEDSMUIR KIRKYARD

Around me wrapped in silence strange and deep
'Neath mounds of green whereon the sunbeams play,
The hillmen rest in God's untroubled sleep,
And glory gilds this sweet autumnal day.

From hills above the purple heather waves
September greetings to the hearts of men.
And gentle Tweed beside these quiet graves
Flows softly in its passage through the glen.

Here at the base of the eternal hills
My soul uplifts the calm expectant prayer
And borne in sweetness from enchanting rills
The Border song fills all the valley there.

And ever more where Tweed and Talla flow
Like guardian angels round these gates of rest,
To keep their tryst the shepherds homeward go
And sleep at last beside the river's breast.

Anon

JOHN DIXON, HILL HERD 1886-1963

A little way beyond the picturesque kirk of Tweedsmuir, in the opposite direction to Moffat, stands the historical sixteenth century Crook Inn, with its charming wrought iron

The historic Crook Inn at Tweedsmuir

embellishments of gambolling lambs and shepherds' crooks.

In the not too distant past the mail coach stopped here on its way to Edinburgh in order to change horses. In 1831 the road was so deep in ruts and quagmire that a traveller residing at the inn took on a wager with the driver that given one hour's start he could be in Edinburgh at the same time as the coach. Such were the conditions that as the driver loosed his horses in Edinburgh, the traveller walked into the coachyard.

At one time the Crook was used as a Presbyterian Meeting House and in 1688 James Thomsone, who became minister of Tweedsmuir, was ordained there. There is little doubt that the inn's sympathy lay with the Covenant, one landlady giving sanctuary within a peat stack to a hunted hillman while the dragoons were served inside with refreshment.

A highly acclaimed descendant of Renwick the Covenanter, the writer and poet John Dixon, alias 'Brockie', 'Hill Herd', or 'Border Herd', dwelt at Stanhope only a stone's throw from The Crook.

His hirsel stretched from the summit of Dollar Law to the banks of the Tweed. He stated that the view he got from Dollar Law, 'couldn't be beat'. Born at Carsphairn in Galloway in 1886, John Dixon was a practical man who remained strong in his belief that a hill ewe should be able to fend for herself.

Six feet tall, he herded some 25 score 'Blackies' at Stanhope, on some 1500 rugged acres. Over a period of 42 years John served under five different employers, each time being taken on along with the sheep.

In winter, wearing a wool balaclava that he himself had knitted, he wrote inspiring prose on scraps of paper as he walked the hill, copying them out in a more professional

The charming wrought iron embellishments of the Crook Inn

manner on reaching home. His feelings for the sheep in his care best personified in the poem he wrote entitled *Our Auld Pet Ewe*.

Auld Moss you noo are deid and gane;
Near by, the Tweed I've laid your frame,
But lang your memory will remain
Fresh tae us a',
And oft we'll speak and praise your name
Tho' you're awa.

I mind as weel that sunny day,
In May of nineteen twenty-twae.
I got you on the Lang-grain-brae
Wi' hunger pressed,
And brocht you hame your pangs to stay
Below my vest.

The twinning season being bye,
For milk you must depend on kye,
And Mr Findlay said if I
Could keep you livin'
That tae the weans we could rely
You wad be given.

It took some care, you were so weak,
Some thocht you'd never turn a sheep;
But critics a' you sair did cheat
And timely grew
Wi' frame and fleece, and horns complete,
A bonny ewe.

You never couped upon your back,
Nor yet a year a lamb did lack,
But every time did make a tap
O' highest grade:
And proved a credit tae the stock
Where you were bred.

Twice ower the nicht was dark and late-
When Tweed cam' doon wi' angry spate
Till haughs and fields were like the lake
Of Galilee-
We thocht that this had sealed your fate
And you maun dee.

But no, you held ticht by the dyke
Till storm and flood were past their height,
And at the break of morning light,
Though some were doomed,
Untae the first bare know in sight
You bravely soomed.

But there's a time by Fate decree't,
That comes alike to folk and sheep,
When freenship's ties, how ever sweet,
Are rent in twain,
As each in turn, in last lang sleep,
Are gathered hame.

In this I hae some consolation,
No torturing pangs of inflammation;
Nor days nor weeks of desolation
Did rack your braith,
But something of a short duration
'Tween health and daith.

Your wee twin lambs you left behind,
Have foster-mothers leal and kind,
And in the fields some pleasure find
Where lang you grazed,
And thochts of you, frae youthfu' minds,
May be erased.

But they who reared you as a pet,
Your pawky wiles will ne'er forget;
How oft you met them at the yett
And ocht wad riskit
Up tae the hoose, wi' them to get
To beg your biscuit.

Now Tweed her course may calmly steer,
Or ower her banks in wrath career,
'Twill not disturb you sleeping near,
In last repose,
Though ower your grave her waters clear
In torrent flows.

A last fare-weel, wee Mossilee,
Your bonnie face nae mair we'll see,
But what 'mang stocks o' pedigree
I come across:
Nae sheep to me will dearer be
Than you, wee Moss.

George Burnett in conversation with John Dixon. Excerpt from *Companion To Tweed*, Methuen and Co. Ltd. 1938.

John is one of four shepherds on the 6000-acre farm of Stanhope. About two thousand black-faced sheep are grazed, each having a theoretical allowance of three acres. In richer country they talk about so many sheep to the acre, but in Tweeddale the problem is acres to the sheep. Drift, a loose handful of black and white energy, which the town-dweller might think dear at ten shillings, floated round our legs as he saw us take the Glen. So keen was he to be at the sheep that no one would have supposed he had run his 25 to 30 miles in the morning.

'How do you train them?' I asked John.

'Different folk hae different ways, so I can only gie my own opinion. A puppy should be spoken to and handled a bit, as soon as it sterts running about, but not petted. It will soon ken its name, and come up to you when cried at. It can then be learned to lie down, when it is told. As soon as it is able to follow to the hill, let it go where it will see older dogs working, but I don't let it chase them. It should not be encouraged or tried to work till it makes a shape of its own free will. When it does run at sheep, unless it is going to abuse them, don't shout or threaten it, but watch what it means tae dae. At that stage if it gets frightened it may never stert again. No dog will ever be a right success unless it has confidence in the man it follows. If a young dog has the right instinct, it wants past the sheep.'

'Like Drift,' I suggested, looking up the hill-side at a wisp of 10 or 15 sheep.

When he heard his name spoken, the dog darted into our line of vision, turning his head with eager jerks to see what his master intended. John raised his crook and Drift shot through the heather and bracken-swift, straight, and clean as a shuttle. The slope of Stanhope Glen is sharp and broken in places with primeval scree, but Drift sped into the distance untiredly. Before he had got up to them, the sheep left nibbling the heather and turned about to look at the dog as if they were seeing him for the first time. Drift sank on his haunches, a little from them, as if he too had happened on a new creation. But the game of staring each other out is not played in Tweeddale.

He drove the sheep at a gentle run to within 200 yards of where we stood. 'Come awa' to me!' Drift detached himself from the sheep like a falling stone, and padded obediently at our heels. After this difficult run his body showed no signs of distress. Only his loop of red tongue vibrated quickly, was momentarily swallowed, and vibrated again. He did not expect his master to pat him on the head and call him a 'good dog', though I thought he deserved it. 'How long will he be able to do this?' I asked.

'Dogs are at their best between two and five,' I was told. 'As a rule they're not much good after eight, though I've one down bye, the mother of this yin, who at 10, is as keen at the runnin' as ever she was. But it's sair wark on the hills, and the rough heather and stanes are hard on their feet.'

'When they get too old?' I asked. 'Oh, then we sell them or gie them awa' to a lowland farmer. Though sometimes,' John added, reflectively, 'the dogs dinna understand the new words of command, and are little use.'

The herd has respect and affection for his dogs, but he does not allow himself or others 'to make a fuss' of them. The collies are his partners in an arduous task and to be useful they must be hard and stout-hearted. So unaccustomed are they to the touch of human hands that they will bite in circumstances that would make the house-dog wag his tail in delight. This is the reason probably for the supposition that collies are treacherous. They are, in fact, entirely faithful and careful — fanatically careful — of their master's property. They will, for example, lie for many hours beside a lambing bag that has been put down and temporarily forgotten, and with equal solicitude, snarl at and bite the shepherd's daughter when she visits her parents after a prolonged period of absence.

At the entrance of the Glen are the owner's house, the farm-steading, and two herds' houses looking starkly across Tweed at the Wormal (1776ft), a hill which is pierced by the longest tunnel of the Edinburgh Corporation's water line from Talla. The traveller who thinks the scene rather desolate should note that a five minutes walk will bring him to the main road between Edinburgh and Moffat, with buses to carry him in either direction, and that Stanhope Burn provides, and has been providing for several years, power for electricity to light the lonely houses and cook meals. About a mile up the glen is another herd's cottage which does not enjoy these advantages, and beyond that there is no other habitation.

Apart from the human and animal interest of the stells, (round or T-shaped) and the faulds or fanks (where the herds keel the sheep and spean the lambs), Stanhope Glen is a broken bit of creation. Here and there a few stunted trees crouch from the wind, giving some idea of what great parts of the forests of Caledon and Ettrick looked like in the days of the Romans down to the later Stuarts. No other forest will arise until the sheep have gone, for in these spare solitudes every green thing is cropped to its root, save the bracken alone. After a time of stress, the sheep continue feeding in the gleam of the cold winter snow, so desperate is the problem of living. In a day or two — doubtless they know it — they may be swirled down the rocky funnels of the hills into the quieter but more dangerous valley. It is then that the herd must bend his strength against the blast, to gather his sheep into the stells, and rake the burns for the unfortunate.

Those that fall in an awkward posture may be 'perished' in a minute or two. Others live beneath the wreaths of snow for many days. In a storm several years ago, the black Sunday and Monday of recollection, a ewe survived under the snow at Tweedsmuir for six weeks. In bad years the floor of John Dixon's cottage may be covered with half-perished lambs, placed there in the hope that the heat of the fire will bring them round. One after the other they stagger to their feet and set up such a baa-ing that, exhausted though they are, neither he nor his wife can sleep for the sound. In the morning all have to be fed with cow's milk, the 30 or so of them needing a cow to themselves which means that humans make shift with water.

Bad weather is ill-fortune at any time, but worst of all at lambing time. Some ewes leave their lambs and the poor innocents are found sucking at heather bushes. Or lambs die and the disconsolate ewes go looking for them. Then those with two must part with one, the skin of the dead being put on the back of the living so that the ewe can smell at least part of her own.

In snow, gale, flood and sunshine the year brings its special work. The quietness of the back-end, if the weather is hospitable, the rush of lambing, with an 18 to 20 hour day; the clipping; the keeling to distinguish the hirsels; the nicking of the horns to show the age of the sheep; the dipping; the warfare on the maggot; the perpetual perambulation of the hills. The last means a steady walk of 20 to 24 miles a day, with about three times that distance for the dogs. In the morning the herd takes the hill to drive the sheep down from the heights where they have passed the night; in the afternoon and evenings he travels the valleys to send them away from the waters and up the hill-side where they spend the night.

The shepherd has no fixed hours. He works to his sheep; only they can tell him what to do. His responsibility, therefore, is complete. The calling needs, for its successful prosecution, self-sacrificing men whose bodies can scarcely be tired; bodies that can endure the changes of temperature incidental to the seasons and those hourly fluctuations caused by rapid descents and ascents to the sheep. For many days in the year they are soaked to the skin with rain, or frozen to the bone with wind and driving snow. Little wonder that elderly herds in Tweeddale suffer from rheumatism, no matter what care they took of themselves in youth. Their feet are their fortune. So they pay great attention to them buying (as a rule) only hand-made boots, which are turned up at the toes for easier walking on the hills. These boots, at current prices, cost 50 shillings a pair and every herd has two pairs. (At today's prices the same pair of boots would cost upwards of £60.)

But these physical attributes would avail little were they not directed and controlled by a rare temper of mind. Nothing matters to the good shepherd except the well-being of his master's sheep. When prices for wool and lambs are good he rejoices with his master; when they are bad he examines himself on the conduct of his hirsel and will go to extreme lengths in observation and study to make things better. But underneath this solicitude for his master is an endearing love of sheep. Herds cannot be improvised. Either they have or do not have the hereditary instinct and knowledge.

As we walked back through the glen, my strides making two to John's one, the breath of the hills and the spirit of the men who spend their lives on them filled me with a great pride. Drift, no doubt feeling the same in his doggie way, took a last look into the broken ground to make sure the sheep were on the upward move. He did not need to be told anything. Man and dog exchanged glances; that was all. The hills closed behind us in the gloaming. The whirr of the grouse and the cry of the curlew suggested that nature was glad to be left alone for the night.

'And how would you like to be a shepherd?' Mrs Dixon asked me over a table laden with cheese scones and all the food that tastes best after a day on the hills.

How indeed would I like to be a shepherd!

7
TRAINING FOR WORK

We are given to understand that the domestic dog can be divided into four main groups, each of these descended from individual wolf ancestry. Over the centuries these groups have been interbred with the idea of improving existing strains. It is obvious, however, to those with a keen eye to attribute the various present day breeds back to their origin. Peoples of a stone-age culture are thought to have been the first to domesticate wolves. At a much later period both Vikings and Romans brought their guarding herding dogs with them when they invaded Britain.

Golden and red coat colouring is a feature of the Aureus species of wolf. The northern wolf, Canis Lupus, is the ancestor of the husky, which in Greenland and northern Russia is being bred back to him in order to strengthen existing strains.

Bearded and shaggy-coated dogs are said to be of mixed ancestry, derived from mastiff and other northern types, developed in the Russian Steppes by shepherds. The narrower skull of our present day collie is attributed by some to an infusion of sighthound blood.

There are those who would argue that today's Border collie is better than it has ever been. It is certainly more suited to present day conditions; with the days of the drover fast receding into the mists of time his dog has been replaced by motorised transport and that of the shepherd is being partially substituted by portable pens and men who excel mainly as motor-bike jockeys.

As the trial field increasingly becomes the shop window of the world, initiative is being replaced by subservience. Gone is the one man dog of days gone by.

I am often asked what the advantages are of owning a smooth-coated dog. Apart from the convenience of short hair I believe these dogs throw back to more practical ancestors. Work, after all, must come first.

Sheep dog handlers have never been more skilled. Scottish handlers regularly bring out nursery dogs that are tuned to perfection with their dignity intact. Apart from the time taken and the professionalism involved, I much prefer a slower approach that allows the dog where possible, to develop naturally under its own steam.

These days, to a certain degree, my heart has gone out of trialling. Flanking a dog here, there and everywhere on unmanageable sheep, decidedly goes against the grain. Admittedly, I felt less guilt when compensation in the way of a visit to the hill where my dog could be left to his own devices was freely on offer. Participation in sheep dog demonstrations provides a measure of consolation, and although these cannot replace the informality and relaxation experienced on the hill, at least they can be flexible in content.

For me there could never be another Bowmont or the privilege of owning a hill dog like Garry. How grateful I am that the two came together. The pleasure that memory conjures up in regard to those 'visits' cannot compare with anything I have yet experienced, when, with stick in hand and Garry scouting ahead, I would walk purposely over the springy turf, revelling at the sound of skylarks and the roar of the rushing burn, to where I could observe my dog's careful work over the steep terrain at least a mile away.

Faithful, constant, resolute, steadfast and true. All these

qualities pertain to loyalty, the mastiff's celebrated virtue. I value loyalty above most other sheep dog traits if it is coupled with sensitivity and determination.

I believe a sensitive collie to be more receptive; however, too large a dosage of sensitivity is undesirable, as is an animal considered by its owner to be 'too clever'. The latter is frequently guilty of anticipating commands even before they are given. This can prove annoying, especially on a trial course where hurdles must be negotiated.

Training a sheep dog can be compared with driving a high-powered car. One must know instinctively when to accelerate and when to apply the brakes. The misguided believe that the finely tuned trial dog is merely a step away from the 'green' young pup at home in the kennel. There are phases almost too numerous to divulge in between — and no short cuts. Most important, the trainer must be prepared to adapt to the individuality of each dog, being in the immortal words of James Gardiner, 'careful not to blunt the genius of the pupil by over direction'.

At all cost emotions must be held in check; any hint of irritation must be banished from the voice and replaced with encouragement. After a period of months, if all else fails anger may be communicated by voice tone and body movement.

Young dogs readily respond to sound rather than to the spoken word. An immediate reaction can be expected if the dog has been addressed and handled in a quiet manner from puppyhood. Puppies must be spoken to constantly, using a persuasive, reassuring tone.

Youngsters should not be chastised too severely for grabbing wool. An adult dog that refuses to catch and hold a sheep is next to useless to a hill shepherd at lambing time.

The importance of working a young dog close at hand

over a period of many months cannot be over-emphasised.

In my present capacity I am frequently asked how shepherding humans compares with shepherding sheep. My standard reply is that sheep don't ask questions. Actually, speaking to people throughout the day can prove mentally exhausting, whereas handling the woolly variety is predominantly physical. All in all, dealing with either species can be rewarding, providing they co-operate.

I firmly believe that the most beneficial relationships develop between people and dogs of a similar temperament. It is much more probable that a boisterous dog will reach its full potential in the hands of an extrovert. Among working breeds, it is those with co-operative natures that are of most benefit, a willing disposition being a much valued attribute. The average shepherd is more than satisfied if his dog meets him halfway. Occasionally a dog or bitch appears on the horizon that is noted for giving 100%. Several years ago my husband owned such an animal in Jan, alias 'The Bionic Bitch'. My young dog Glen, being a direct descendant, never ceases to amaze me with his enthusiasm.

We must never under any circumstances underestimate the perception of our forebears, to whom necessity was very much the mother of invention. I feel nothing short of admiration regarding our predecessors, whose intuitive examples still bear fruit. For example, the Border collie is a result of countless generations of careful breeding: method, initiative, loyalty, even colouring and texture of coat were carefully evolved in this herding athlete.

The past centuries have produced a wide variety of herding types, depending on the conditions they were required to work in.

The shepherd's mastiff was originally bred to ward off dangerous predators — both animal and human — and at a

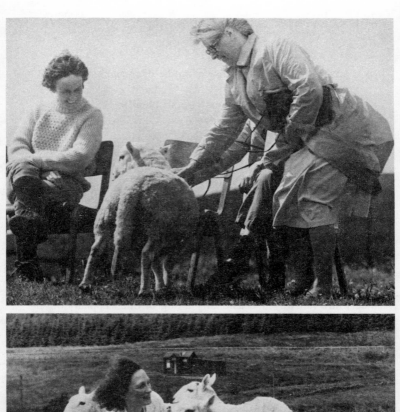

Top: *Shepherding humans*. Bottom: *Shepherding sheep*

later date to guard precious kale-yards. A 'heavy steady' type was used in-bye for folding flocks on root crops, while agile lighter-framed beasts with a natural cast, were preferred in hilly and mountainous regions to gather the wild forest sheep. All of these varieties were employed by drovers to move sheep and cattle the length and breadth of Britain.

North of the Border, the collie has long been the shepherd's right arm, as well as his bread and butter. When seeking employment a useful dog or dogs has always been a requirement. (We have Iris Combe, in her thoroughly researched book entitled *Herding Dogs*, to thank for finally providing a feasible derivation of the word 'collie', as meaning 'useful' in the common Gaelic, known as Q Celtic.)

Although least mentioned in its history, the woollen industry owes much to the accomplishment of the shepherd's dog.

At no other time has such interest been generated world-wide, regarding Border collies; they are regularly featured in books, on video, through the press and television — the fascination spreads. Britain's ambassadors are not only two-legged, the versatile shepherd's dog skilfully performs its duties on the trial field and with the world's vast flocks.

Our puppies and trained dogs are sold to working homes only. They first see the light of day in the nursery, where they are born onto a wooden bench covered by clean sacking.

Solid food is introduced when the puppies are three weeks old. They are dosed for round worms one week later and again at six weeks.

The 'nest' space is gradually increased until after

Glen, left, Geoff and Holly

weaning at the age of seven weeks they are given the run of the byre; clean sawdust is provided daily and wooden sleeping benches are a permanent feature.

The pups are kept inside until fully inoculated; they are handled daily, spoken to regularly and kept free from vermin.

Once they are three months old those that are kept for our own use are taken out twice a day for exercise with the older dogs; at this stage they are taught their names and to come quickly when they hear a soft, repetitive whistle. Very occasionally on these walks, I give the older dogs a 'stop whistle'. The attending youngsters, seeing their elders freeze, invariably follow suit. This is termed 'backing' by the gun dog fraternity. It is a natural reaction inherited from wild ancestors so as not to disturb prey.

By six months of age the pups are on one meal a day having gone from two when they were given as much as they could eat. They are now at an age to move in with an adult group. Living loose inside a large building within a family environment, they appear not only content but also secure. They look forward eagerly to their outings, endeavour to please and on their return have ample opportunity to contemplate what they have learned. By this time they have been introduced to sheep, usually at around the age of four months. On these excursions they are accompanied by an older dog to prevent mishaps. Once an initial reaction to the sheep is observed I shush the pup on to encourage it to head the sheep. At this stage it is beneficial to use an experienced dog to drive the sheep in the opposite direction so that the pup's natural instinct to head be aroused.

Over the following several months the puppies are taken to see sheep two or three times a week. On arrival, the first few minutes are spent having fun, allowing both the pup and the sheep to rid themselves of over-exuberance. Working regularly in rough undulating terrain on free moving sheep helps the dog gain confidence as well as encouraging it to give room on the corners and to cast naturally on the outrun. Rarely during these excursions is the pup's method of working interfered with. On occasions we take the flock walkabout, deliberately encountering all kinds of hazards such as gateways, bridges, woodland and water.

By the time that the dog is a year old all manner of nice moves are beginning to develop. It is relatively easy to create situations whereby commands can be fitted to what the dog is actually doing, rather than insisting he obeys for no apparent reason. This approach leads to a happy, trusting and unquestioning relationship.

He should be asked to stand, rather than to lie down, then, providing he is not inclined to flatten to the ground be allowed to choose his own position. It is important that initially the outrun and fetch are left to the dog, so that he develops the habit of both bringing the sheep to you and fetching them in a straight line. A dog that is not over-endowed with determination quickly learns to keep his distance; others must eventually be taught to take time. At this stage it is beneficial if voice intonation and accentuated body movement are used by the trainer — canines being very much in tune to both — because it is the method they use to communicate with one another in the wild. It is no use using a quick sound or movement if a slow reaction is required. For example, a fast whistled or spoken command encourages a dog to move quickly, while slowly given instruction accompanied by a leaning of the handler's body illustrates steadiness and wide movement. At approximately

14 months of age the handler can begin to teach the dog to work in gears rather than continually stopping and starting him. Some trainers give the appearance of being rooted to the spot. They should be prepared to run down the field, if necessary.

Above all else, I have learned that when dealing with collies, nine times out of ten, if you do the opposite to what your inclination dictates, you will be right.

Usually I teach the stop command when the pup is actually working with the sheep. In this situation he is stopping for a valid reason — eye tiredness, sheep in a corner — all of these circumstances can be used to convey what the command to stop requires.

To encourage a dog to flank I walk around a sizeable flock shushing him on ahead. After flanking both left and right a number of times I invite the pup to continue round behind me, using the same 'come here' whistle I use on our walks. This exercise ensures that eventually the dog will be able to be placed anywhere. Too much of this can, however, cause the dog to forget where the point of balance or heavy-side of the flock is. Therefore, depending on how naturally free the dog is, the exercise must be accompanied by an equal amount of working the sheep in the handler's direction without commands.

Both driving and shedding are accomplished by inviting the dog through a large gap in the flock. The shed sheep can then be driven by the trainer and the dog until the penny drops and the dog takes the sheep on unaided. Should the dog show reluctance to remain between the shed sheep and the rest of the flock, the handler should move quickly on in front, encouraging his pupil to bring the sheep after him. After a time or two this ploy will no longer be necessary. The importance of not 'overfacing' a young dog

The 'skin-head' variety

at this stage cannot be over emphasised. Patience and understanding are imperative or a dog may be ruined, regarding shedding, for life.

Depending on the individual, dog training can be extremely time-consuming, taking a great deal of thought as well as patience. I have heard handlers confess to sleepless nights, worrying how a problem has arisen and more important, how they are going to cure it.

After training a number of dogs of varied temperaments a natural feel develops. Above all else, the teacher learns self-control, for without it no progress will be made.

When all the necessary attributes are present in the pupil, training is quickly and easily accomplished and is a pleasurable task. Should the pupil be particularly intuitive a kind of primitive and beautiful ballet can develop with the whistles and verbal commands sung as an accompaniment.

It should be mentioned that keeping the dog on form once training is accomplished is infinitely more difficult. A confident, happy and respectful working relationship will only be perpetuated by a considerate master.

WINTER '89

Other than Garry and Laddie, all my dogs are smooth-coated. I have undergone a complete reversal in my preference for the 'skin-head' variety, as young Geoff amusingly describes them.

I lay the blame for this complete turnabout squarely at Holly's paws. At three years old and the mother of 18 children — all replicas of herself — she has developed into a solid bundle of muscle whose quiet purposeful method of working reminds me more of Old Meg, Garry's grand-

Holly and friends outside The Wee School

mother, as each day passes.

Throughout the summer her leisure time is spent welcoming individual cars as they pull into the parking area, then, acting as officiator and guide, encouraging the occupants, willing or not, in the direction of the demonstration area in order to show off her prowess.

Her children and grandchildren can truly be termed, international jet-setters with four of them already gracing the sheep walks in America and Canada. A daughter from Holly's first marriage follows in the pawprints of the dogs of James Hogg, the famed nineteenth century Ettrick Shepherd, at Mountbenger.

In between working and canvassing Holly is at her happiest when exercising her strong maternal instinct. Last spring I stood in amazement while she washed the face of a baby lamb before retrieving it from the burnside. I have observed her top and tail new-born kittens as gently as though they were her own.

Young Glen, Holly's eldest son, has developed into a strapping replica of his mother. When off duty he exhibits a pointer's continually flaying stern. When working, although likened to quick-silver, he is a good stopper, dropping like a stone on hearing my whistle.

When caught in sunlight his smooth coat gleams like jet; there are, believe it or not, varying shades of black. His powerful chest, graceful neck and strong limbs are white as the driven snow. Physically he is a perfect specimen with high shoulder blades and the shadow of well sprung ribs, portraying an athlete's fitness.

Character-wise, I would describe Glen as a 'fun dog', exhibiting a wealth of humour. His countenance is ugly-beautiful, his expression dominated by enormous ears — the right pointing skyward, the left, as yet undecided.

Holly

When breeding smooth on smooth some interesting characteristics emerge. For instance, Glen's skull is an entirely different shape and considerably broader than either Garry's or Laddie's, and his lower front teeth protrude slightly forward like those of a mastiff.

I find that puppies from Holly and Cap have an above average pack instinct with a strong urge to quarter the ground; in fact, they are true hunters and huntresses. I have witnessed Holly's whelps gather a full-grown hind from the forest and bring it unharmed to my feet. They also possess an extremely keen attitude to work and are much faster and more precise than their hairy equivalents. Most of them come ready-made requiring little or no training, which suits my present life-style perfectly.

Although greyhound and pointer blood is obvious in their make-up, the mastiff's loyalty predominates. Glen's lavish show of affection warms me through and through. He is constantly checking on my whereabouts during our numerous forays and is a ferocious guard should a strange dog approach. He shows endearment by leaning heavily against my legs like a cat, gazing up at me with affectionate dark eyes.

Besides being presented to Her Majesty the Queen when she visited the Scottish Borders in 1988, both Holly and her offspring have been featured in a number of TV productions. These include the BBC children's programme *Caterpillar Trail*, BBC Two's farming programme *Landward*, ITV's *Landmark*, BBC Two's, *The Animals Road-Show*, where she was filmed suckling her latest litter of six puppies as well as five of her grandchildren, and recently with son Glen, on ITV's *Blind Date*, hosted by Cilla Black.

A couple of years before our move to Tweedhopefoot, I was invited along with Garry, Laddie and some ducks to

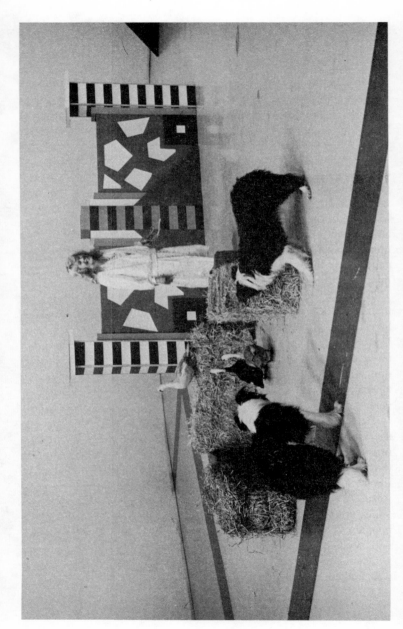

Viv duck-herding on the set of the BBC programme Blue Peter

travel to London, in order that we might appear on the children's programme *Blue Peter*. We set off from the railway station at Berwick-upon-Tweed at the crack of dawn, with the three ducks safely incarcerated in a large, yellow, plastic box, tightly fastened with string.

Shortly before we reached London, a city gent, complete with briefcase and bowler, boarded the train. He chatted politely for a few minutes, suspiciously eyeing the box from which faint scratching noises could be heard. Finally, curiosity got the better of him and he asked what was inside. I couldn't resist the temptation of telling him a little white lie and said, the box contained a large python and that I was an erotic dancer.

Conversation ceased immediately and he hurriedly edged away. After one or two suspicious glances in our direction, he proceeded to read his newspaper. When it came time for us to alight, he looked across at me and said in a rather puzzled tone: 'Don't you mean an exotic dancer?'

I decided to tell him the truth at which he roared with laughter, picked up the box and carried it along the platform for me.

There was more fun to come. After I arrived at my destination one of the ducks laid an egg which, when the box was tipped up to release them, rolled from one side of the television studio to the other.

Over the past two years I have lost count of the number of people who confided: 'We owned a Border collie but we had to have it destroyed.' Equally alarming were the never-ending requests from those outside of farming who wished to purchase a Border collie puppy.

Towards the conclusion of each sheep dog handling demonstration it is our practice to release a portion of the younger untrained dogs, from four months of age upwards, in order that the public may observe their inherent ability. On leaving the kennels, these older puppies race pell-mell in the direction of the demonstration area, very often leaping the garden fence in the process. So great is their desire to reach the sheep that they totally ignore the onlookers. However, the moment that the sheep are removed to an adjoining paddock these youngsters bound gleefully in the direction of the visitors, who in return make much of their presence.

I use this occurrence as a living example as to why these dogs should not be removed from their natural environment. Furthermore, I deplore the practice of farmers who breed them purely for the pet market.

Border collies, because of their intelligence, attractive appearance and the glamour that surrounds them, have become popular in all walks of life, as rescue dogs, on the show bench and in obedience and agility.

Selection has ensured that some possess an amenable nature, however, it should be remembered that first and foremost the Border collie is a sheep herding dog, carefully evolved by drovers, shepherds and farmers. In the wrong hands, due mainly to its abundant vitality and strong herding instinct, it can become a lethal weapon. It is for these reasons and because of the consequences that our dogs are sold to shepherds and farmers only.

The following paragraphs are written with the genuine notion of assisting collie owners outside the farming and trialling fraternity to develop a better understanding of their dog's requirements.

Border collie puppies should not be fed on too high a protein diet. Neither should they receive too much in the way of exercise at an early age. Both these circumstances, I am convinced, can cause hip and other major bone deformities.

In Britain, young sheep dogs are allowed to mature and develop slowly, like a good tup horn or a keg of wine — the reason being that one does not set a boy to do a man's job.

Too high an intake of protein can cause aggression. Possibly because of financial reasons, many shepherds feed their dogs on a low protein diet of around 20%. It is mostly racing greyhounds and breeds of a similar energy output that are fed until the steam comes out of their ears.

Contrary to the layman's belief, other than at busy times, for example gatherings and lambings, a good stockman walks quietly among his flock, gaining much satisfaction from studying them at their ease, his dog ranging carefully ahead, causing just enough disturbance in order to ascertain the unsound from the sound sheep.

Such is the trust generated because of this regular gentle behaviour on the part of the shepherd and his dog that the sheep barely pause in their never-ending task of subsistence, other than to bleat a muffled welcome.

On the far-side of the Atlantic 'hyper' is an oft used expression in regard to the Border collie. Diet may be a contributory factor, but the reason is more likely to be a lack of understanding resulting in a form of breakdown on the part of the animal — perhaps more common than realised — because the amount of pressure tolerated by the individual varies from dog to dog. The attendance of 'clinics' or 'training seminars' can contribute detrimentally to a young dog's mental state. In Britain it is considered unwise to take a dog away from home until it is capable of running in an open trial.

To expose an immature youngster to the antics of its contemporaries for hours on end while awaiting its turn of assessment and subsequent correction can only be described as unsettling to say the least.

In theory I believe the clinic to be a sensible idea; it is the lack of consideration to dogs and especially to sheep, at some events, that I deplore.

Discussions regarding any subject are bound to be rewarding. I believe tuition to be more beneficial if given at home in familiar surroundings.

Surely it would considerably simplify matters if the instructor were to demonstrate the prowess of his own dogs of various ages and stages so that any problems could then be given an airing.

I was appalled to learn that shock collars are used by some individuals in order to gain their dog's attention. Apart from the obvious callousness involved, these people are defeating the object of the exercise. I maintain that prevention is always better than a cure and have yet to meet a collie dog that if bred, reared and trained in the correct manner, presented a serious problem. It should be remembered, however, that restriction almost always produces an adverse reaction when dealing with an animal that has been bred to exercise initiative.

To the owners of show Border collies and those used in obedience, contrary to what others advise, I would suggest strongly for the sake of their dogs that they endeavour to breed the working instinct out as quickly as possible.

COLLIE'S LAMENT

I am a well-bred collie dug,
Born tae herd yon hill.
Tae rin, tae head, jeukin' yowes,
Yet ne' er do them ill.
Alas, the worst tae me's occurred,
A' ve bin selt intae a toon,
And 'cos I chase baith weans and cars,
They're gang tae pit me doon.
If I could talk I'd tell them,
I wasna' born to be a pet —
But they dinna appear to care nor ken,
Jest drag me tae the vit.
I don't know what he did tae me,
'Cept 'twas a mortal sin,
That made me proud tae be canine,
Not human loikes o' him.
How I wished that he'd explain,
To they foolish toonie folk
An;' mak' 'em onderstand,
That a collie dug born an' bred,
Belongs only on the land.
But alas, he only sighed
And shook his woolly head,
Carried oot the heinous deed
And then pronounced me deid!

I feel mysel' ascendin',
Towards some pearly gates —
A' ve bin telt a shepherd dwells up there
Who waits for collies syke as me.
I tak' ma place beside his knee,

Feel his kind hand on my head,
'Forget the past, put it behind,
Come bide with me instead.
There's sheep to guide and sheep to shed,
The work here never ends.'
He led me tae a dry-stane dyke,
'These are the ones ye'll tend.'
I stood and eyed in mute surprise
Across the heaven's deep
As what I deemed were wisps of cloud
Developed intae sheep.
And not the sort one wad expect,
For I couldna' fail tae see
The sheep the good shepherd tended o'er
Were of the human variety.
Observing ma perplexed gaze, he inquired:
'Do you stand firm as the proverbial rock?'
I wagged ma tail — so, with a quiet 'wheep',
He sent me off in hot pursuit
To educate His flock.

8

PASTORAL ANECDOTES

SHEEP: Taken from *The Ettrick Shepherd's Tales Vol II*

The old black-faced or Forest breed have far more powerful capabilities than any of the finer breeds that have been introduced into Scotland. So strong is the attachment of sheep to the place where they have been bred, that I have heard of their returning from Yorkshire to the Highlands. I was always somewhat inclined to suspect that they might have been lost by the way. But it is certain, however, that when once one, or a few sheep, get away from the rest of their aquaintances, they return homeward with great eagerness and perseverance. I have lived beside a drove-road the better part of my life, and many stragglers have I seen bending their steps northward in the spring of the year. A shepherd rarely sees these journeyers twice; if he sees them, and stops them in the morning, they are gone long before night, and if he sees them at night, they will be gone many miles before morning. This strong attachment to the place of their nativity is much more predominant in our old aboriginal breed, than in any of the other kinds with which I am acquainted. The most singular instance that I know of, to be quite well authenticated, is that of a black ewe that returned with her lamb from a farm in the head of Glenlyon to the farm of Harehope in Tweeddale, and accomplished the journey in nine days. She was soon missed by her owner, and a shepherd was dispatched in pursuit of her, who followed her all the way to Crieff, where he turned and gave her up. He got intelligence of her all the way, and everyone told him that she absolutely insisted in travelling on — she would not be turned, regarding neither sheep nor shepherd by the way. Her lamb was often far behind, and she had constantly to urge it on by impatient bleating. She unluckily came to Stirling on the morning of a great annual fair, about the end of May, and judging it imprudent to venture through the crowd with her lamb, she halted on the north side of the town the whole day, where she was seen by hundreds, lying close by the road-side. But next morning, when all became quiet, a little after the break of day, she was observed stealing quietly through the town, in apparent terror of the dogs that were prowling about the streets. The last time she was seen on the road was at a toll-bar near St Ninian's; the man stopped her thinking she was a strayed animal, and that someone would claim her. She tried several times to break through by force when he opened the gate, but he always prevented her, and at length she turned patiently back. She had found some means of eluding him, however, for home she came on a Sabbath morning, the fourth of June, and she had left the farm of Lochs in Glenlyon, either on the Thursday afternoon, or Friday morning, a week and two days before. The farmer of Harehope paid the Highland farmer the price of her and she remained in her native farm till she died of old age, in her seventeenth year.

A shepherd in Blackhouse bought a few sheep from another in Crawmell, about 10 miles distant. In the spring following, one of the ewes went back to her native place, and yeaned on a wild hill called Crawmell Craig. One day, about the beginning of July following, the shepherd went out and brought home his ewe and lamb — took the fleece from the ewe and kept the lamb for one of his stock. The lamb lived and throve, became a hogg and a gimmer, and never offered to leave home; but when three years of age, and about to have her first lamb, she vanished; and the morning after, the Crawmell shepherd, in going his rounds, found her with a newly-yeaned lamb on the very gair of the Crawmell Craig, where she was lambed herself. She remained there till the first week of July, the time when she was brought a lamb herself and then she came home with hers of her own accord: and this custom she continued annually with the greatest punctuality as long as she lived. At length her lambs, when they came of age, began the same practice, and the shepherd was obliged to dispose of the whole breed.

One of the two years while I remained on this farm, (Willenslee) a severe blast of snow came on by night about the latter end of April, which destroyed several scores of our lambs; and as we had not enow of twins and odd lambs for the mothers that had lost theirs, of course we selected the best ewes, and put lambs to them. As we were making the distribution, I requested of my master to spare me a lamb for a hawked ewe which we knew, and which was standing over a dead lamb in the head of the hope, about four miles from the house. He would not do it, but bid me let her stand over her lamb for a day or two, and perhaps a twin would be forthcoming. I did so, and faithfully she did stand to her charge; so faithfully, that I think the like never was equalled by any of the woolly race. I visited her every morning and evening and for the first eight days never found her above two or three yards from the lamb; and always, as I went my rounds, she eyed me long ere I came near her, and kept trampling with her foot, and whistling through her nose, to frighten away the dog; he got a regular chase twice a day as I passed by: but, however excited and fierce a ewe may be, she never offers any resistance to mankind, being perfectly and meekly passive to them.

The weather grew fine and warm, and the dead lamb soon decayed, which the body of a dead lamb does particularly soon; but still this affectionate and desolate creature kept hanging over the poor remains with an attachment which seemed to be nourished by hopelessness. It often drew the tears from my eyes to see her hanging with such fondness over a few bones, mixed with a small portion of wool. For the first fortnight she never quitted the spot, and for another week she visited it every morning and evening, uttering a few kindly and heart-piercing bleats each time; till at length every remnant of her offspring vanished, mixing with the soil or wafted away by the winds.

James Hogg

During the spring and summer I myself was witness to a similar heart rending incident on the road to Moffat. A bonny Blackfaced ewe, with a strong pair of cross Suffolk lambs, would insist on grazing the grassy banks on either side of the road. Often I admired them as I drove by. However, one morning, much to my regret the finest lamb lay dead, killed by a vehicle of some sort or another, its dam standing over it with hanging head, while her other offspring grazed nearby. One week later I was greatly surprised to find her still at the same spot, even though the carcass had long-since been lifted. She continued there, feeding in that same area, until taken home at weaning time some five months later.

WYLIE
by Dr John Brown (1860)

Our next friend was an exquisite shepherd's dog; fleet, thin
flanked, dainty, and handsome as a small greyhound, with
all the grace of silky waving black and tan hair. We got her
thus. Being then young and keen botanists, and full of the
knowledge and love of Tweedside, having been on every
hill top from Muckle Mendic to Hudleshope and the Lee
Pen, and having fished every water from Tarth to Leithen,
we discovered early in spring that young Stewart, author of
an excellent book on natural history, a young man of great
promise and early death, had found the *Buxbaumia Aphylla*,
a beautiful and odd-looking moss, west of Newbie heights,
in the very month we were that moment in. We resolved to
start next day. We walked to Peebles, and then up Haystoun
Glen to the cottage of Adam Cairns, the aged shepherd of
the Newbie hirsel, of whom we knew, and who knew of us
from his daughter, Nancy Cairns, a servant of uncle Aitken
of Callands. We found our way up the burn with difficulty,
as the evening was getting dark; and on getting near the
cottage heard them at worship. We got in, and made
ourselves known, and got a famous tea, and such cream and
oat cake! — old Adam looking on us as 'clean dementit' to
come out for 'a bit moss,' which, however, he knew, and
with some pride said he would take us in the morning to the
place. As we were going into a box bed for the night, two
young men came in, and said they were 'gaun to burn the
water.' Off we set. It was a clear, dark, starlit, frosty night.
They had their leisters and tar torches, and it was something
worth seeing — the wild flame, the young fellows striking
the fish coming to the light — how splendid they looked
with the light on their scales, coming out of the darkness —

the stumblings and quenchings suddenly of the lights, as the torch-bearer fell into a deep pool. We got home past midnight, and slept as we seldom sleep now. In the morning Adam, who had been long risen, and up the Hope with his dog, when he found we had wakened, told us there was four inches of snow, and we soon saw it was true. So we had to go home without our cryptogamic prize.

It turned out that Adam, who was an old man and frail, and had made some money, was going at Whitsunday to leave and live with his son in Glasgow. We had been admiring the beauty and gentleness and perfect shape of Wylie, the finest colley I ever saw, and said, 'What are you going to do with Wylie?' 'Deed,' says he, 'I hardly ken. I canna think o' sellin' her, though she's worth four pound, and she'll no like the toun.' I said, 'Would you let me have her?' and Adam, looking at her fondly — she came up instantly to him, and made of him — said, 'Aye, I wull, if ye'll be gude to her;' and it was settled that when Adam left for Glasgow she would be sent into Albany Street by the carrier.

She came, and was at once taken to all our hearts — even grandmother liked her; and though she was often pensive, as if thinking of her master and her work on the hills, she made herself at home, and behaved in all respects like a lady. When out with me, if she saw sheep in the streets or road, she got quite excited, and helped the work, and was curiously useful, the being so making her wonderfully happy. And so her little life went on, never doing wrong, always blithe and kind and beautiful. But some months after she came, there was a mystery about her: Tuesday evening she disappeared; we tried to watch her, but in vain, she was always off by 9pm; and was away all night, coming back next day wearied and all over mud, as if she had travelled far. She slept all next day. This went on for some months, and we could make nothing of it. Poor dear creature, she looked at us wistfully when she came in, as if she would have told us if she could, and was especially fond, though tired.

Well, one day I was walking across the Grassmarket, with Wylie at my heels, when two shepherds started, and looking at her, one said, 'That's her; that's the wonderfu' wee bitch that naebody kens.' I asked him what he meant, and he told me for months past she had made her appearance by the first daylight at the 'buchts' or sheep-pens in the cattle-markets, and worked incessantly, and to excellent purpose, in helping the shepherds to get their sheep and lambs in. The man said with a sort of transport, 'She's a perfect meeracle; flees about like a speerit, and never gangs wrang; wears but never grups, and beats a' oor dowgs. She's a perfect meeracle, and as soople as a maukin.' Then he related how they all knew her, and said, 'There's that wee fell yin; we'll get them in noo. 'They tried to coax her to stop and be caught, but no, she was gentle, but off; and for many a day that 'wee fell yin' was spoken of by these rough fellows. She continued this amateur work until she died, which she did in peace.

BIRKIE

It is very touching the regard the south-country shepherds have to their dogs. Professor Syme one day, many years ago, when living in Forres Street, was looking out of his window, and he saw a young shepherd striding down North Charlotte Street, as if making for his house: it was midsummer. The man had his dog with him, and Mr Syme noticed that he followed the dog, and not it him, though he contrived to steer for the house. He came, and was ushered into his room; he wished advice about some ailment, and Mr Syme saw that he had a bit of twine round the dog's neck, which he let drop out of his hand when he entered the room. He asked him the meaning of this, and he explained that the magistrates had issued a mad-dog proclamation, commanding all dogs to be muzzled or led on pain of death. 'And why do you go about as I saw you did before you came into me?' 'Oh,' said he, looking awkward, 'I didna want Birkie to ken he was tied.' Where will you find true courtesy and finer feeling? He didn't want to hurt Birkie's feelings.

THE FLESHER'S DOG: Taken from *The Ettrick Shepherd's Tales Vol II*

The late Mr Steele, flesher in Peebles, owned a bitch whose feats in taking home sheep from the neighbouring farms and into the market at Peebles by herself, form innumerable stories in that vicinity, all similar to one another. But there is one instance related of her, that combines so much sagacity with natural affection, that I do not think the history of the animal creation furnishes such another.

Mr Steele had such an implicit dependance on the attention of this animal to his orders, that whenever he put a lot of sheep before her, he took a pride in leaving it to herself, and either remained to take a glass with the farmer of whom he had made the purchase, or took another road, to look after bargains or other business. But one time he chanced to commit a drove to her charge at a place called Willinslee, without attending to her condition, as he ought to have done. This farm is five miles from Peebles, over wild hills, and there is no regularly defined path to it. Whether Mr Steele remained behind, or took another road, I know not; but on coming home late in the evening, he was astonished at hearing that his faithful animal had never made her appearance with the drove. He and his son, instantly prepared to set out on different paths in search of her; but on their going out to the street, there she was coming with the drove, no-one missing; and, marvellous to relate, she was carrying a young pup in her mouth! She had been taken in travail on the hills; and how the poor beast had contrived to manage her drove in her state of suffering, is beyond human calculation; for her road lay through sheep the whole way. Her master's heart smote him when he saw what she had suffered and effected; but she was nothing daunted; and having deposited her young one in a place of safety, she again set out full speed to the hills and brought another, and another, till she brought her whole litter, one by one; but the last one was dead.

I give this as I have heard it related by the country people, for though I knew Mr Walter Steele well enough, I cannot say I ever heard it from his own mouth. I never entertained any doubt, however, of the truth of the relation, and certainly it is worth being preserved for the credit of that most docile and affectionate of all animals — the shepherd's dog.

SIRRAH

My dog was always my companion, I conversed with him the whole day — I shared every meal with him and my plaid in the time of a shower; the consequence was that I generally had the best dogs in all the country.

The first remarkable one that I had was named Sirrah. He was beyond all comparison the best dog I ever saw. He was of a surly unsocial temper — disdained all flattery, and refused to be caressed; but his attention to his master's commands and interests never will again be equalled by any of the canine race.

The first time that I saw him, a drover was leading him in a rope; he was hungry and lean, and far from being a beautiful cur, for he was all over black, and had a grim face striped with dark brown. The man had bought him off a boy for three shillings, somewhere on the Border, and had doubtless used him very ill on his journey. I thought I discovered some sort of sullen intelligence in his face, not withstanding his dejected and forlorn situation; so I gave the drover a guinea for him, and appropriated the captive to myself. I believe there never was a guinea so well laid out; at least I am satisfied that I never laid out one to so good purpose. He was scarcely then a year old, and knew so little of herding, that he never turned sheep in his life; but as soon as he discovered that it was his duty to do so, and that it obliged me, I can never forget with what anxiety and eagerness he learned his different evolutions. He would try everywhere deliberately, till he found out what I wanted him to do; and when once I made him understand a direction, he never forgot or mistook it again. Well as I knew him, he very often astonished me, for when hard pressed at accomplishing the task he was put to, he had expedients of the moment that bespoke a great share of the reasoning faculty. Were I to relate all his exploits, it would require a volume; I shall only mention one or two to prove what kind of an animal he was.

I was sent to a place in Tweeddale, called Stanhope, to

bring home a wild ewe that had strayed from home. The place lay at the distance of 15 miles and my way to it was over steep hills, and athwart deep glens — there was no path, and neither Sirrah nor I had travelled the road before. The ewe was brought in and put into a barn overnight; and, after being frightened in this way, was set out to me in the morning to be driven home by herself. She was as wild as a roe, and bounded away to the side of the mountain like one. I sent Sirrah on a circular route wide before her, and let him know that he had the charge of her. When I left the people at the house, Mr Tweedie, the farmer, said to me: 'Do you really suppose you will drive the sheep over these hills, and out through the midst of all the sheep in the country?' I said I would try to do it. 'Then, let me tell you,' he said, 'that you may as well travel to yon sun.' The man did not know I was destined to do one and the other!

Our way, as I said, lay over wild hills, and through the middle of flocks of sheep. I seldom got a sight of the ewe, for she was sometimes a mile before me, sometimes two; but Sirrah kept her in command the whole way — never suffered her to mix with other sheep — nor, as far as I could judge, ever to deviate 20 yards from the track by which he and I went the day before. When we came over the great height towards Manor Water, Sirrah and his charge happened to cross it a little before me, and our way lying downhill for several miles, I lost all traces of them, but still held on my track, I came to two shepherds' houses, and asked if they had seen anything of a black dog, with a branded face and a long tail, driving a sheep? No, they had seen no such thing; and besides, all their sheep, both above and below the houses, seemed to be unmoved. I had nothing for it but to hold on my way forward; and, at length, on the corner of a hill at the side of the water, I discovered my trusty coal-black friend sitting with his eye fixed intently on the burn below him, and sometimes giving a casual glance behind to see if I was coming: he had the ewe standing there, safe and unhurt.

When I got home and set her at liberty among our own sheep, he took it highly amiss. I could scarcely prevail with him to let her go; and so dreadfully was he affronted, that she could have been let go free after all his toil and trouble, that he would not come near me all the way to the house, nor yet taste any supper when we got there. I believe he wanted me to take her home and kill her.

Whenever Sirrah found himself hard set, in commanding wild sheep on steep ground, where they are worst to manage, he never failed, without any hint to the purpose, to throw himself wide in below them, and lay their faces to the hill, by which means he got the command of them in a minute. I never could make Hector (Sirrah's son) comprehend this advantage, with all my art, although his father found it out entirely of himself. The former would turn or wear a sheep no other way, but on the hill above them; and though very good at it, he gave both them and himself double the trouble and fatigue.

It will appear strange to hear a dog's reasoning faculty mentioned, as it has been; but I have hardly seen a shepherd's dog do anything without perceiving his reasons for it. I have often amused myself in calculating what his motives were for such and such things, and I generally found them very cogent ones. But Hector had a droll stupidity about him, and took up forms and rules of his own, for which I could never perceive any motive that was not even farther out of the way than the action itself. He had one uniform practice, and a very bad one it was, during the time of family worship, that just three or four seconds before the conclusion of prayer, he started to his feet and ran barking around the apartment like a crazed beast. My father was so much amused with this, that he would never suffer me to correct him for it, and I scarcely ever saw the old man rise from prayer without his endeavouring to suppress a smile at the extravagance of Hector. None of us could ever find out how he knew that the prayer was near done, for my father was not formal in his prayers; but certes he did know — of that we had nightly evidence. There never was anything for which I was so puzzled to discover a reason as this: but, from accident, I did discover it, and, however ludicrous it may appear, I am certain I was correct. It was much in character of many of Hector's feats, and rather, I think, the most outre of any principle he ever acted on. His chief daily occupation was pointing the cat. Now, when he saw us all kneel down in a circle with our faces crouched on our paws, in the same posture with himself, it struck his absurd head, that we were all engaged in pointing the cat. He lay on tenters all the time, but the acuteness of his ear enabling him, through time, to ascertain the very moment when we would all spring to our feet, he thought to himself: 'I shall, be the first after her for you all!'

The most painful part of Sirrah's history yet remains; but in memory of himself, it must be set down. He grew old, and unable to do my work by himself. I had a son of his coming up that promised well, and was a greater favourite with me than ever the other was. The times were hard, and the keeping of them both was a tax upon my master which I did not like to impose, although he made no remonstrances. I was obliged to part with one of them; so I sold old Sirrah to a neighbouring shepherd for three guineas. He was accustomed, while I was shearing, or doing any work about the farm, to go with any of the family when I ordered him;

and run their bidding the same as at my own; but then, when he came home at night, a word of approbation from me was recompense sufficient and he was ready next day to go with whomsoever I commanded him. Of course when I sold him to this lad, he went away when I ordered him, without any reluctance, and wrought for him all that day and the next as well as he ever did in his life. But when he found that he was abandoned by me, and doomed to be the slave of a stranger for whom he did not care, he would never again do another feasible turn. The lad said that he ran among the sheep like a whelp, and seemed intent on doing them all the mischief he could.

The consequence was, that he was obliged to part with him in a short time; but he had more honour than I had, for he took Sirrah to his father, and desired him to foster him, and be kind to him as long as he lived, for the sake of what he had been; and this injunction the old man faithfully performed.

He came back to see me now and then for months after he went away, but afraid of the mortification of being driven from the farmhouse, he never came there; but knowing well the road that I took to the hill in the morning, he lay down near to that. When he saw me coming he did not venture near me, but walked round the hill, keeping always about 200 yards off, and then returned to his new master again, satisfied for the time that there was no more shelter with his beloved old one for him. When I thought how easily one kind word would have attached him to me for life, and how grateful it would have been to my faithful old servant and friend, I could not help regretting my fortune that obliged us to separate. The unfeeling tax on the shepherd's dog, his only bread-winner has been the cause of so much pain in this respect. The parting with old Sirrah, after all that he had done for me, had such an effect on my heart, that I have never been able to forget it to this day; the more I have considered his attachment and character, the more I have admired them; and the resolution that he took up, and persisted in, of never doing a good turn for any other of my race, after the ingratitude that he had experienced from me, appeared to me to have a kind of heroism and sublimity in it. I am, however, writing nothing but the plain simple truth, to which there are plenty of living witnesses. I then made a vow to myself, which I have religiously kept, and ever shall, never to sell another dog; but that I may stand acquitted of all pecuniary motives — which indeed those who know me will scarcely suspect me of — I must add, that when I saw how matters went, I never took a farthing of the stipulated price of old Sirrah. I have Sirrah's race to this dying day; and thought none of them has ever equalled him as a sheep dog, yet they have far excelled him in all the estimable qualities of sociality and humour.

The statue of James Hogg at St Mary's Loch

9

JAMES HOGG
THE ETTRICK SHEPHERD
(1770-1835)

Since the day that we made our 'epic' journey into Scotland with all our 'goods and chattels' almost 18 years have passed. During that time, great admiration amounting to nothing less than hero worship has developed regarding the two great bards of the last century, namely James Hogg, the Ettrick Shepherd and his friend Sir Walter Scott of Abbotsford.

Due mainly to the immense pleasure and the immeasurable interest they have given me, I have attempted in the following pages to describe their life-styles. I admit to feeling a special, though humble, affinity with both men — only the passing of time divides us, the rivers and hills remain the same, everlasting memorials to their literary greatness. Because we have shared a similar rustic existence, there are comparisons to be made: for instance, their appreciation of nature's overwhelming beauty, the value they placed on friendship and most important, their obvious enjoyment of social occasions.

Sequences in the following two chapters have been obtained from various biographies.

On turning right at the small village of Tweedsmuir, some six miles north of Tweedhopefoot, one encounters a scenic stretch of road leading towards the A708 and St Mary's Loch, that I for one consider to by-pass some of the most dramatic and delightful scenery in the Scottish Borderland. True, there is an exceedingly awesome mountain to negotiate but the spectacular panorama one beholds on reaching the summit, especially of Talla Water when the sun is going down, makes the hairy ascent well worth the endeavour. The whole inspiring area, with its majestic rolling heather-clad hills, enormous, glistening, grey, water and weather-worn boulders and frothy falls, cascading from hundreds of feet, exudes an ethereal charm that is difficult to fully portray. Who knows, perhaps this engaging retreat is not dissimilar to the one where 'Will O'Phaup', born in 1691, whose real name was William Laidlaw, grandfather of the famous Ettrick Shepherd, first encountered the fairies, or 'little people', as they were oft described. For, 'he was the last man of this wild region who heard, saw and conversed with the fairies and that not once, or twice, but at sundry times and seasons'.

Still further up the glen one beholds the ingenuity of Megget Water, held in check like an unruly child by a giant mother dam, surrounded on higher ground by whitewashed farm houses, the unfortunate originals of which lie buried deep under water keeping company with the once fertile haugh, after which the shimmering loch of St Mary comes quickly into sight overlooked by the inn of Tibbie Shiel's kept in the time of James Hogg by the lady of the same name. Erected nearby as guardian of the lochs stands an impressive memorial to the Borders bard, who would undoubtedly have been proud of such a gesture, even though it came some 25 years after his death. For in the *Noctes Amrosianae* of the famous *Edinburgh Magazine* he expresses the hope that, 'when he is cauld in the moold there may be a bit monument to his memory in some quiet spot fornent Tibbie's dwelling'.

The enormous white stone statue is the work of Andrew Currie of Darnick, sculptor and antiquary, who depicted the shepherd seated as though deep in thought with his collie Hector at his side, and in his hand a scroll bearing the last line of *The Queen's Wake* — 'Have taught the wandering winds to sing'.

It would seem most appropriate that the dog Hector was selected for inclusion in the work; there is strong evidence to suggest that this animal, above all others, held a special affection in his master's heart.

'He (Hector) was the son and the immediate successor of the faithful old Sirrah,' the shepherd wrote, 'and though not nearly so valuable a dog as his father, he was a far more interesting one. He had three times more humour and whim about him; and though exceedingly docile, his bravest acts were usually tinctured with a grain of stupidity. Accordingly', he wrote, 'we went together to the fold to turn out the lambs and there was poor Hector, sitting trembling in the very middle of the fold-door, on the inside of the flake that closed it, with his eyes still steadfastly fixed on the lambs. He had been so hardly set with them after it grew dark that he durst not for his life leave them, although hungry, fatigued and cold, for the night had turned out a deluge of rain. He had never so much as laid down; for only the small spot he sat on was dry and there had he kept watch the whole night. Almost any other collie would have discerned that the lambs were safe enough in the fold, but honest Hector had not been able to see through this. He even refused to take my word for it; for he would not quit his watch, though he heard me calling, both at night and morning.'

But what of honest Hector's master? Perhaps the biographer Veitch provided the most genuine description available… 'When shall we see such another shepherd?' he surmised. 'There is not in all Border history a more complete type of a man of power nourished by the Border glens and streams, haughs and hills, story, ballad, tradition, than he. There is no more complete example anywhere of the rise to intellectual eminence of a nearly entirely self-taught man.'

Much has been written by James Hogg's critics, some good, some bad. Throughout my amateur research, that which overrides all else and therefore boosts the shepherd in my estimation, is his sheer determination to succeed despite all odds, as well as the obvious caring attitude towards his wife, Margaret, and their young family. He suffered and overcame many disadvantages — at one time both he and his dependents being 'left without a sixpence in the world'. During all of this, James remained cheerful; none of his 'reverses' preyed on his spirits. 'I never knew either man or woman who has been so uniformly happy as I have been.' This statement he contributes to 'a sound constitution as well as the conviction that a heavenly gift, conferring the powers of immortal song was inherent in my soul'. And save for some remarkably good days of fishing, shooting and curling on the ice, his marriage was so perfect that he could not separate one from the other. He did not marry until he was nearly 50, which possibly accounts for his obvious appreciation of the 'arrangement' when it came.

He first met Margaret Phillips, his wife-to-be, when living in Edinburgh. She was the sister-in-law of his friend James Gray, of the High School.

James Hogg was born in the year 1770 in the remote and lonely valley of Ettrick. W.S. Crockett, minister of

Tweedsmuir and author of *The Scott Country* gives all the
due credit to the bard's mother, Margaret Laidlaw, for his
later literary success. 'A shepherd's wife assiduous in daily
duty, with a freshness of heart and quickness of head that
brightens toil' is how he described her. Her father, Will,
apart from his conversations with fairy folk, is best
remembered for his great strength and fleetness of foot. His
grandson, being proud of his maternal grandfather's varied
achievements eventually composed the following to be
inscribed on his gravestone. 'Here lyeth William Laidlaw,
the far-famed Will O'Phaup, who for feats of frolic, agility
and strength, had no equal in his day. Born at Craik AD
1691 and died in the 84th year of his age.' Beneath this
inscription: 'Also Margaret, his eldest daughter, spouse to
Robert Hogg and mother of the Ettrick Shepherd. Born at
Old Over Phaup in 1730 and died in the 83rd year of her
age.'

In simpler comparison, the final resting place of their
famous descendent bares the epitaph, 'Here lie the immortal
remains of James Hogg, the Ettrick Shepherd, who was
born at Ettrick Hall in the year 1770 and died at Altrive
Lake, the 21st day of November, 1835.' The original
Ettrickhall (as it is now spelt) was but a stone's throw away
from the kirkyard.

Robert Hogg, James' father, had also begun life as a
shepherd, but by the time of his marriage had saved enough
money to take on the leases of Ettrick House and Ettrick
Hall, afterwards becoming a dealer in sheep, droving many
miles to markets on both sides of the Border. Unfortunately,
owing to a decline in the price of these animals and the
absconding of his principal debtor, he was ruined and
became bankrupt.

'Everything was sold by auction and my parents were

turned out of doors without a farthing in the world,' wrote
James in his memoirs. 'I was then in the sixth year of my
age and remember well the distressed and destitute
condition we were in. At length, the late worthy Mr Brydon
of Crosslee took compassion upon us; and taking a short
lease of the farm at Ettrick House, placed my father there as
his shepherd and thus afforded him the means of supporting
us for a time. This gentleman continued to interest himself
in our welfare until the day of his untimely death, when we
lost the best friend we had in the world.'

'The school,' according to James, 'was almost at our
door.' He attended for a short period of time and was such
an enthusiastic student that he was given the honour of
standing at the head of a juvenile class who read the shorter
catechism and the Proverbs of Solomon.

The following Whitsunday, after the expulsion from the
farm, he was obliged to go into service when only seven
years old, herding cows for a farmer who provided him
with a half yearly wage of 'a ewe lamb and a pair of new
shoes'.

So great was his exuberance that by all accounts he spent
some of his energy running races against time — and
against himself! It was during these exploits that first of all
he lost his plaid, then his bonnet, then his coat and finally
his hosen, for he did not at that time own any shoes. 'In
that naked state did I herd for several days, till a shepherd
and maid-servant were sent to the hills to look for them and
found them all,' James wrote.

The following year, his parents took him home during
the winter quarter and put him to school with a lad named
Ker, who was teaching the children of a neighbouring
farmer. 'Thus terminated my education. After this I was
never another day at any school whatever. In all, I had

spent about half a year at it. I was again, that very spring, sent away to my old occupation of herding cows. This employment, the worst and lowest known in our country, I was engaged in for several years under sundry masters, till at length I got into the more honourable one of keeping sheep.'

He goes on to tell of his admiration for the so-called fairer sex. That same summer, when only eight years old, he was sent out with 'a rosy cheeked maiden' to help her herd a flock of newly-weaned lambs, in addition to the mischievous cows which he had to tend. 'But as she had no dog and I had an excellent one, I was ordered to keep close by her. Never was a master's order better obeyed. Day after day, I herded the cows and the lambs both, and Betty had nothing to do but to sit and sew. Then we dined everyday together at a well near to the Shiel — sikehead and after dinner I laid my head down on her lap, covered her bare feet with my plaid and pretended to fall sound asleep. One day, I heard her say to herself, "Poor little laddie, he's joost tired to death," and then I wept until I was afraid she would feel the warm tears trickling on her knee. I wished my master, who was a handsome young man, would fall in love with her and marry her, wondering how he could be so blind and stupid as not to do it.'

When he was 14 years old James bought himself an old violin for the sum of five shillings saved from his meagre wage. Although he had very little spare time during the day, when not over fatigued he would generally spend an hour or two in the evenings sawing over his favourite Scottish tunes. His bed always being in either stable or cow house, he disturbed nobody but himself and the occupants.

After leaving the farm of Singlee James went to work for Mr Laidlaw at Elibank Upon Tweed, where he found the

situation entirely agreeable. 'I staid there three half-years —
a term longer than usual; and from thence went to
Willenslee, to Mr Laidlaw's father, with whom I served as
a shepherd two years, — having been for some seasons
preceding employed in working with horses, threshing & c.'
It was while working at Willenslee that James, then 20
years old, was given reading matter by his employers wife,
which he read when tending the ewes allowed. These books
were mostly theological. He admits to understanding very
little of the text and that the little that he did understand,
'had nearly turned over my brain altogether. All the day I
was pondering on the grand millennium, and the reign of
the saints; and all the night dreaming of new heavens and a
new earth — the stars in horror and the world in flames!'
Mrs Laidlaw also provided him with newspapers, which he
read diligently.

On Whitsunday in the year 1790, James hired himself to
Mr Laidlaw of Black House, Yarrow, with whom he was
employed as a shepherd for 10 years. He admits to being
treated more as a son than an employee and confesses to the
probability that 'I should have been there still had it not
been for the following circumstance. My brother William
had for some time before occupied the farm of Ettrick
House, where he resided with our parents; but having taken
a wife and the place not suiting two families, he took
another residence, and gave up the farm to me. The lease
expiring at Whitsunday 1803, our possession was taken by
a wealthier neighbour'.

James' first published work, a poem, appeared anonym-
ously in the *Scots Magazine* in 1794, when he was aged 23.
Mr Laidlaw lent him a number of valuable books and no
sooner did he begin to read, than he began to write. For
several years his compositions consisting of 'songs and

ballads made up for the lasses to sing in chorus; and a proud man I was when I first heard the rosy nymphs chaunting my uncouth strains and jeering me by the still dear appellation of Jamie the poeter'.

Having little spare time from his flock, such was his dedication, that he folded and stitched a few sheets of paper, which he carried everywhere in his pocket. He possessed no ink-horn, but in place of one, borrowed a small vial, which he managed to fix into a hole in the breast of his waistcoat and having a cork fastened by twine, it proved satisfactory. 'Thus equipped, whenever a leisure minute or two offered and I had nothing else to do, I sat and wrote out my thoughts as I found them.'

The bard on Ettrick's mountain green,
In nature's bosom nursed had been,
And oft had marked, in forest lone,
Her beauties on her mountain throne;
Had seen her deck the wildwood tree,
And star with snowy gems the lea;
In loveliest colours paint the plain,
And sow the moor with purple grain,
By golden mead, and mountain sheer,
Had viewed the Ettrick waving clear,
Where shadowy flocks of purest snow
Seemed grazing in a world below.

Sir Walter Scott's factor, William Laidlaw, was a boy of 10 in 1790 when James Hogg was employed by his father as shepherd at Blackhouse. James was described at that period in time as, 'rather above the middle height, of faultless symmetry of form and of almost unequalled agility and swiftness. His face was round and full and of a ruddy complexion, with light-blue eyes that beamed with gaiety, glee and good humour — the effect of the most exuberant animal spirits. His head was covered with a singular profusion of light brown hair, which he was obliged to wear coiled up under his hat. On entering church, he used, on lifting his hat to assist with a graceful shake of his head in laying back his long tresses, which rolled down below his loins; and many an eye was turned on him as with light steps he ascended the stair to the gallery, where he sat'.

According to James, the first time that he met Walter Scott was in the summer of 1801. He mentions that he was busy working in the fields at Ettrick House when old Wat Shiel came posting over the water to tell him that there were some gentlemen waiting to see him directly at Ramseycleugh. He had already seen the first volumes of the *Minstrelsy of The Scottish Border* and had sent Scott some ballads for the third volume, furnished by his mother.

On hearing from Wat that he thought it was 'the Shirra an' some of his gang', James threw down his hoe and hastened home to put on his Sunday clothes, but was met on the way by Scott and William Laidlaw.

Margaret Hogg recited the ballad of *Auld Maitland* much to the excitement of those present, then went on to caution the Sheriff with the information that 'there was never ane o' my sangs prentit till ye prentit them yoursel' and ye hae spoilt them awthegither. They were made for singin' an' no' for readin'; but ye hae broken the charm noo, an' they'll never be sung mair. An' the worst of a', they're nouther richt spell'd nor richt setten down'. 'Take ye that, Mr Scott,' said Laidlaw, no doubt with a twinkle in his eye.

Mrs Hogg proved to be right. 'From that day to this, these songs,' commented James, 'which were the amusement of every winter evening, have never been sung more.'

A social evening with Mr Brydon at Ramseycleuch followed, during which there was a prolonged argument as to the profitability of keeping short sheep (the original black-faced forest breed) and long sheep (which were Cheviots). Eventually Scott became tired of the discussion and with tongue in cheek enquired of his host: 'How long must a sheep actually measure to come under the denomination of a long sheep?'

'It's the woo', sir; it's the woo' that mak's the difference,' Brydon divulged. 'The lang sheep hae the short woo' an' the short sheep hae the lang thing, an' these are just kind o' names wie gie them, ye see.'

At this, Scott's face went gradually awry and gave way to a hearty guffaw. Later, Brydon's revelation was to give James the clue to the authorship of *The Black Dwarf* when he perceived these very same words written near the beginning.

Between the years 1801 and 1810, James' life seems to be unsettled to say the least. He had by then known some measure of success due to his writing, but all of his farming ventures had unfortunately failed. Everything was taken by his creditors and he discovered much to his chagrin that no-one, because he had been a farmer, would employ him as a shepherd. He tells us that, finally in the month of February, 1810, 'in utter desperation, I took my plaid about my shoulders and marched away to Edinburgh, determined, as no better could be, to push my fortune as a literary man'. He was at that time 40 years old and fortunately for him had two good friends living in the city, Scott and Grieve, who were hatters by trade. He was able to lodge with them for a six month period and they not only helped him with money and clothes, but were able to provide him with numerous beneficial acquaintances. One of these being the

Short sheep at the Grey Mare's Tail

aforementioned James Grey, brother-in-law to James' future wife, Margaret, whom he had to wait 10 years to marry because of his unreliable source of income.

In the summer of 1810, he published *The Forest Minstrel* and dedicated this work to the Duchess of Buccleuch. Next, on September 1, 1810, came *The Spy*, a weekly newspaper edited and written mostly by himself. In the third and fourth numbers, the printing of what in those days was considered to be a risque tale, lost him half his readers. *The Spy* finally folded after only 52 editions had been published.

In his younger days James was a member of a literary society and through it learned much. In Edinburgh, together with some others, he formed the Forum, a debating society. The public were charged sixpence for admittance and the meetings were held weekly for a period of three years.

In 1811 James was persuaded by Grieve to return to poetry and the preparation for publication of *The Queen's Wake*. This work, published in 1813, proved to be James' most enterprising attempt so far. He walked about the city gazing into shop windows, seeking his book but not liking to enquire of its popularity, until by chance he met William Dunlop, a whisky merchant, who assured him he had finally, 'hit the right nail on the head', and that 'the new beuk had cheated him out of a night's sleep.'

There were those of course, who insisted that 'it was impossible for a work of such excellence to be accomplished by a man who had actually spent the greater part of his life in the character of a shepherd'.

From that day onwards, James' popularity rose like a flood-tide.

It was around this time, from 1812 to 1813, that he made the acquaintance of John Wilson. He was so taken with the descriptiveness of his *Isle of Palms*, that he was anxious for a meeting with the author. This proved difficult, as all he could learn of him was that 'he was a man from the mountains of Wales, or the west of England, with hair like eagles' feathers and nails like birds' claws, a red beard and an uncommon degree of wildness in his looks'. Eventually, James managed to discover his whereabouts and invited him to dinner. 'I found him so much a man according to my own heart, that for many years we were seldom twenty-four hours asunder when in town. I afterwards went and visited him, staying with him a month at his seat in Westmorland, where we had some curious doings among the gentlemen and poets of the lakes.' Wilson dwelt at Elleray, overlooking Lake Windermere.

In *Noctes Ambrosianae*, the dialogues first published in William Blackwood's *Edinburgh Magazine*, James is introduced to the readers in the character of a shepherd. 'Noctes', a mixture of truth and fiction, were largely the works of John Wilson writing under the pseudonym of Christopher North.

Wilson, Lockhart and James Hogg were the original 'leading lights' of Blackwood's monthly magazine. The first edition appeared on April 1, 1817, but after three months the editors, Pringle and Cleghorn, went over to a rival magazine, taking the list of subscribers with them. This 'rival' subsequently collapsed, whereupon Mr Blackwood, with the invaluable assistance of Hogg, Wilson, Lockhart and R.P. Gillies, became his own editor and within a short space of time an article appeared in the magazine, entitled 'Translation From an Ancient Chaldee Manuscript'.

There is no doubt that James was responsible for penning most of this 'revelation'. Mr Blackwood had been strongly against publishing the piece, but was persuaded by the others, who added 'a good deal of deevilry of their own'. (The original having been much less defamatory.)

The article, not surprisingly, caused an uproar throughout the city of Edinburgh. Blackwood was eventually prosecuted and was ordered to pay £1000 in damages and costs. Bad publicity being eminently more desirable than no publicity, the magazine got off to a flying start, with its writers supplying as much sensationalism as they could muster.

Between 1819 and 1822, when the first of the Noctes appeared, Wilson gradually took over as editor with Blackwood assuming the function of business manager. The Noctes featured James in a far from flattering role. Sir George Douglas writes in the shepherd's defence: 'In these celebrated dialogues, the principal part was borne by the Shepherd. The situation thus brought about was probably unique in literature, for here was a writer of established reputation, made to figure month after month as the mouth-piece of remarks and opinions of which he had generally as little previous knowledge, as any other member of the public.'

On a number of occasions, James had reason to be genuinely offended by the articles written about him, though on the whole, he took it in good part. However, when a particularly insulting review of *The Mountain Bard* appeared in Blackwood's, James was justifiably peeved.

In 1828, by then a happily married man with a young family, his patience once again was wearing thin. He wrote Blackwood, 'I am exceedingly disgusted with the last beastly "Noctes" and as it is manifest that the old business of mocking and ridicule is again beginning, I have been earnestly advised by several of my best and dearest friends to let you hear from me in a way to which I have a great aversion. But if I do, believe me it shall be free of all malice and merely to clear my character of sentiments and actions which I detest and which have proved highly detrimental to me.'

Feeble attempts were made both by 'North' in the Noctes and Lockhart, writing in the *Quarterly Review*, to pacify James. The wound proved deep and for a space of time he was conspicuous by his absence. In May of 1834 he is welcomed back with 'hurrahs'.' The Shepherd swears that the past is forgotten and that he will never breathe a word of any misunderstanding. 'North' he forgives absolutely and from then on continues to be the hero of the Noctes until his death in 1835. His staunch young wife, however, could never listen to the Noctes descriptions of her husband without exhibiting 'heightened colour and every sign of lively indignation'.

James dedicated his work *The Forest Minstrel* to the Duchess of Buccleuch. In March of 1814 he wrote her a letter acknowledging that he had received on more than one occasion 'her private bounty' and requesting the continuance of her patronage. He goes on to say that there is a small farm on her estate that would be suitable for his ageing parents, both of whom are upwards of 84 years, and himself to reside in. Five months later the Duchess died and her husband, to whom she had mentioned the matter, felt obliged to carry out her wishes and offered James the farm of Altrive in Yarrow at a nominal rent.

In 1820 James married Margaret Phillips. She was 30 and he was almost 50. He had given her the choice of two days, both surprisingly close. The knot was tied on April 27 in Dumfries, followed next morning by a religious ceremony at Mouswald.

Margaret had until that date lived with her parents and an unmarried sister. Her father was a well-to-do farmer and cattle dealer who owned a number of farms in Dumfriesshire.

Mouswald Place, east of Dumfries, was in those days considered to be of mansion proportions, therefore there is every likelihood that the couple's lengthy courtship was due to James' feelings of inadequacy. Finally, in March of that year he considered the small but comfortable Altrive worthy enough of a lady of Margaret's standing and his future prospects sufficiently encouraging to warrant the marriage taking place. Following the religious ceremony at Mouswald, the happy couple left the same afternoon for Moffat in a hired chaise, completing the journey to Yarrow the following day by gig, a vehicle more suited to the hilly terrain.

Blackwood's magazine referred to the wedding in the following way: 'The marriage took place in Dumfriesshire, at the house of the bride's father and there also the happy pair remained till next morning. The transition to Ettrick was performed on the morrow by the principal personages in four gigs. The first gig contained Mr and Mrs Hogg, the best man and the best maid occupied the second gig, the third was filled by the two Messrs Brydon, and in the fourth sat the shepherd's faithful black servant in a new suit of the Hogg livery.' (As this gentleman is never again mentioned it is suggested that he was borrowed for the occasion.)

'They dined at the cottage of Altrive and next day the solemn kirking took place at Yarrow kirk, the minister choosing for his text the following passage: "Blessed is the man whom thou honourest and causest to approach unto thee." Seriously I am rejoiced to hear of my worthy friend's excellent fortune — he has married, according to

every account, a most amiable, prudent and intelligent
woman — and may he be as happy with her (his best friend
could say nothing more strongly) as he deserves. I hope,
however, his domestic felicity will form no obstacle in the
way of his literary labours... and of the silent but sure
progress of his fame.'

The newly married couple received a letter of congratu-
lations from Sir Walter Scott, mentioning the 'pleasant loss'
of his elder daughter, Sophia, in marriage to John Lochart.

Margaret quickly settled down to her new life, by all
accounts the only grievance being that Altrive boasted no
spoons other than those made from horn!

'A promised visit to Edinburgh did not materialise. The
couple were far too busy socialising.

'He (James) has cut Edinburgh entirely... let him have
his new mahogany tables and black hair-cloth sofa in good
condition and stock well that cozie cupboard in the corner,
dispensing liquid sweets — for it is thirty-three miles good
(over the hills from Peebles) and there is nothing more
dangerous than to drink cold water after a long walk in
summer,' enthused *Blackwood's* in May of 1820.

James, also politely turns down an invitation from John
Wilson to attend his first lecture as Professor of Moral
Philosophy given at the University of Edinburgh. He has by
then an even better excuse for remaining at home for
Margaret is expecting a child. Eventually, in the spring of
1821 the visit is accomplished and their first borne, a son
named James Robert, is delivered by Dr Crighton, a friend
of the family, on March the 21.

In 1812 Peter Phillips, Margaret's father, had made a
will bequeathing £1000 to each of his surviving daughters.
On the promise of the advancement of this sum for the
purchase of livestock and the knowledge that there was

money owing to him from various publishers, James felt confident enough in taking a nine year lease on Mountbenger, a much larger farm bordering Altrive, knowing that the property had already ruined two farmers in the space of six years.

By then both his parents were dead and he had no dependents other than his wife and young son. In April 1821, owing to a severe misfortune, Margaret's father suffered a major financial loss, in short he was ruined and unable to provide the promised £1000. Thus the situation was reversed and James found himself benefactor to the Phillips, a role he took on willingly. At this point there was still time for James to pull out of the Mountbenger lease. However, driven by an overwhelming desire to farm successfully and the fact that he now had a son to carry on the tradition, he foolishly threw caution to the wind taking possession at the May term, while continuing to live at Altrive. At that time a severe agricultural depression, after the prosperity of the Napoleonic wars, was already being felt, which became more serious as time went on. His publishers, on whom he depended, refused to acknowledge their debts, Blackwood being one of the main offenders!

It was around this time that Sir Walter suggested that James accompany him to London to attend the Coronation of George IV and in the hopes of improving his (James') fortunes. The date of the Coronation was set for July 18. Saint Boswell's Fair, where James intended purchasing 500 hoggs, was to take place on the 17th.

'Reluctantly — after giving the offer much thought, sometimes with the tear in my eye', James decides to attend the fair.

The ensuing years were filled with both exhausting physical labour on the farm and during any spare moment, exacting literary work in order to make ends meet.

Another happy event occurred in the spring of 1823 when Margaret gave birth to a daughter, proving that these difficult exacting times, were not without their moments.

James adored children and was eventually to father five, one boy and four girls.

The following is an extract from his *Familiar Anecdotes of Scott* describing Sir Walter's elder daughter: 'Sophia was a baby when I first visited him, about two or three months old and I have watched her progress ever since. By the time she had passed beyond the years of infancy I perceived that she was formed to be the darling of such a father's heart and so it proved. She was a pure child of nature without the smallest particle of sophistication in her whole composition. And then she loved her father so. Oh how dearly she loved him! I shall never forget the looks of affection that she would throw up to him as he stood leaning on his crutch and hanging over her at the harp as she chaunted to him his favourite old Border ballads or his own wild Highland gatherings. Whenever he came into a room where she was, her countenance altered and she often could not refrain from involuntary laughter.'

Regarding Sir Walter's attitude towards the Hogg siblings, James wrote of an occasion when his son James took the bard's attention, endeavouring to discover what was in the boy by asking him a number of simple questions, not one of which James would answer. 'He then asked me anent the boy's capabilities. I said he was a very amiable and affectionate boy but I was afraid he would never be the ''Cooper of Fogo'' for he seemed to be blest with a very thick head.' ''Why, but Mr Hogg you know it is not fair to lay the saddle upon a foal,'' said he. ''I for my part never liked precocity of genius all my life and can venture that

James will yet turn out an honour to you and all your kin.''
I was gratified by the prediction and lost not a word of it.'
(In fact James Hogg junior lived up to expectations and
eventually became a banker.) Mrs Hogg was also apparently
a favourite of Sir Walter's, he paying her the greatest
deference and attention. 'As for the poor woman,' James
wrote, 'she perfectly adored him. There was one day when
he was dining with us when, on going away, he snatched up
my little daughter, Margaret Laidlaw, and kissed her, and
then laying his hand on her head, said: ''God Almighty
bless you my dear child!'' On which my wife burst into
tears. On my coming back from seeing him into the carriage
that stood at the base of the hill I said, ''What ailed you
Margaret?'' ''Oh,'' said she, ''I thought if he had but just
done the same to them all I do not know what in the world
I would not have given!'''

Relationships between the two bards were not always
harmonious. Regarding James' prose, Sir Walter was
equally capable of criticism, be it intended as constructive,
or otherwise. There is no doubt that plagiarism occasionally
occurred or rather 'tit for tat'.

On one occasion a heated argument sprang up regarding
comparisons between their works, namely the Shepherd's
Brownie of Bodsbeck and Sir Walter's rendering of *Old
Mortality*. James rose intending to leave in a huff. 'No, no,
stop!,' cried Sir Walter, 'you are not to go and leave me in
bad humour. You aught not to be offended at me for telling
my mind freely '

'Why to be sure,' James replied, 'it is the greatest folly
in the world for me to be sae. But ane's beuks are like his
bairns, he disna like to hear them spoken ill o', especially
when he is conscious that they dinna deserve it.'

Instances such as these only serve to portray the more

human aspects of their characters, thus making them all the more endearing. Their final get together took place in the autumn of 1830, two years before Sir Walter's untimely death. They met at the Gordon Arms on the way to Yarrow. 'He sent me word,' wrote James, 'that he was to pass on such a day on his way from Drumlanrig Castle to Abbotsford. I accordingly waited at the inn and handed him out of his carriage. His daughter was with him, but we left her at the inn and walked slowly down the way as far as Mountbengerburn. He then walked very ill indeed, for the weak limb had become almost completely useless; but he leaned on my shoulder all the way and did me the honour of saying, he never leaned on a firmer or a surer. We talked of many things, past, present and to come, but both his memory and onward calculation appeared to me to be then considerably decayed. I cannot tell what it was, but there was something in his manner that distressed me. He often changed the subject very abruptly and never laughed. He expressed the deepest concern for my welfare and success in life, more than ever I had heard him do before, and all mixed with sorrow for my worldly misfortunes. There is little doubt that his own were then playing on his vitals. When I handed him into the coach that day, he said something to me which, in the confusion of parting, I forgot and though I tried to recollect the words the next minute, I could not and never could again. It was something to the purport that it was likely it would be long 'ere he leaned as far on my shoulder again, but there was an expression in it, conveying his affection for me, or his interest in me, which has escaped my memory for ever.'

In 1824 Margaret's aged parents had come to live at Altrive, while the obliging Hogg family crossed over the water to take up residence at Mountbenger. Three years

later, Peter Phillips died and his widow moved into
Mountbenger for the remaining few months that were left to
her.

The lease on the farm was up at Whitsuntide (May 15,
1830), James was then 60 years old. In 1827 he wrote that
he was liable for arrestment — no doubt due to debt. That
he managed to hold on to the farm until the out-going says
much for the leniency of his creditors and his own
determination. James wrote that Margaret remarked that she
had forgotten the time she had money in her pocket, to
which he replied that he had just one shilling in his
possession and that it had remained so long a solitary
resident that he thought it would be a lucky one. The April
of 1827 appears to have been a gruelling one with many
farmers losing as many as 100 sheep out of every thousand.
Fortunately for James, although he lost beyond his
proportion of lambs, thankfully all his ewes weathered the
storm.

In 1828 he wrote Blackwood: 'I wish you would send
me some pens and ink, for you may see I'm unco ill
hadden. I hae na' had a pen this year, but puing ane out o'
the clocher gooses wing, or the gainders ance a month and
my ink is a little gun powder and soot mixt wi' water. '

As the time to vacate Mountbenger loomed closer, James
lamented that he was to be stripped of everything — his
precious books, his silver bowl. Fortunately, circumstances
did not warrant such a loss. His most treasured possessions
exist to this day in New Zealand, along with his writing
desk, inherited by his descendants. (Oh that they had
remained in the land of his birth!)

James sold up at a loss, although the sale was considered
a good one under the circumstances. 'With young Buccleuch's lenience there will be but little loss. He has acted

nobly and could do no more in the present circumstances, for he sent orders to the factor to drop all claims whatever on the heavy arrears and not to suffer one thing of Hogg's to be rouped, either out of doors or within doors, on his account.'

James vowed to live a sober sportless life, but within a month of returning to Altrive he was able to visit Edinburgh, one of many future excursions. He had thankfully never been more popular as a writer. Towards the end of 1831 however, there occurred the most fierce disagreement yet with Blackwood regarding the postponement of the publication of his *Altrive Tales*. In the latter part of November, James received a letter from Blackwood written in a very bad humour stating that he would neither advance him money on the work that had lain a year unpublished, nor commence a new work in a time of such agitation — and that he must not think of it for another year at least. James suspected that the whole pretence was a ploy to prevent him from going to London, which he had proposed visiting, thus keeping him within the publisher's own jurisdiction.

It was James' hope that the publication of *Altrive Tales* would provide security for his family after his death. On December 6 James sat down and wrote one of his 'terrible letters' breaking off all literary connections with Blackwood. By then Blackwood was himself suffering from ill-health and appeared not to care one way or the other, regarding the outcome. James had asked for no reply to his letter and received none. 'A young London publisher, named Cochrane, seemed disposed to regard a writer's wishes' — and it was to him that James offered his manuscript. On December 22 he was making preparation to set sail on The Edinburgh Castle. He arrived in London on

December 31, 1831, after a somewhat slow and tedious voyage. The following day he wrote Margaret saying he had seen both Cochrane and Lockhart and that the Locharts were in deepest distress, regarding the death of little Johnnie.

Almost from the moment of landing, James was 'like to be eaten up with kindness'. He began working with Cochrane, but was disturbed to hear that his 'new publisher' was venturing beyond his means.

In one of his letters, James confided that he hated London, 'notwithstanding all the caressing I have met with, which is perfectly ridiculous. It is almost a miracle that I keep my health so well, considering the life I lead, for I am out at parties every night until far in the morning. I am sure I have received in the last three days, three hundred invitations to dinner and I am afraid I have accepted too many of them.'

'I do not think that either flattery or profit can ever make me love it (London). It is so boundless that I cannot for my life get out of it, nor can I find any one place that I want.' He complains in a further correspondence that the sight of piles of dead larks in the markets cause him immeasurable distress.

During his visit, Thomas Carlyle, as yet to build his reputation as a writer, described James as 'a little red skinned stiff sack of a body with quite the common air of an Ettrick shepherd' — the Londoners had specifically asked that he wear his plaid and blue bonnet — 'except that he has a highish though sloping brow, (among his yellow grizzled hair) and two clear little beads of blue or grey eyes that sparkle, if not with thought, yet with animation. Behaves himself quite easily and well; speaks Scots, and mostly narrative absurdity.' He goes on to say: 'All are bent

James Hogg, the Ettrick Shepherd (1770-1835)

on bantering him, especially Lockhart, Hogg walking through it as if unconscious, or almost flattered. His vanity seems to be immense, but also his good nature.' (James never did endeavour to disguise his vanity, wearing it as armour.) 'I felt interest for the poor "herd-body", wondering to see him blown hither from his sheepfolds and how quite friendless as he was, he went along cheerful, mirthful and musical.'

Carlyle ended his impression: 'Is the charm of this poor man chiefly to be found herein, that he is a real product of nature and able to speak naturally, which not one in a thousand is? An unconscious talent; though of the smallest, emphatically naive. Once or twice in singing (for he sung of his own) there was an emphasis in poor Hogg's look — an expression of feeling, almost of enthusiasm.'

On January 22, Margaret told James in a letter that few people approve of London at first. She believed that one must stay awhile to become fond of it, but begged James to leave before he became too fond of it. 'Leave before you are threadbare,' she pleaded. 'I do not exactly mean your coat, but leave the Londoners something to guess at. By the bye, the coat is no joke either, for you are apt to wear it too long, but take care, don't do so, buy a good new one and whatever articles of dress you may require. By no means appear shabby — you went so hurriedly, there was no time to prepare for so long a journey, I should rather wear a worse gown, than that you should appear in a shabby coat, you must get your stockings and other things mended by the person who washes your clothes, it is pitiful to think of you going about with great holes in your stockings. I hope you have got warm drawers and do by all means attend to your health, you know I often tell you, you abuse a good constitution, when I think of your late, or rather, early hours, I am perplexed about you. I know you cannot stand it — this is really almost a curtain lecture,' Margaret apologises. In another letter she implored her husband: 'I beg you will write often, at least once a week. James begs you will come home. He gets no sport without you.'

In reply: 'I dined with Sir George Warrender the other day, with two Earls, two Lords and seven Scottish Baronets and felt just as much at home as if I had been at Sundhope or Whitehope. The drawing-room chairs were all gilded and covered with blue satin and there were six mirrors that reached from the ceiling to the floor, so that I felt in spite of all I could do, as if I had been in a small drawing room, in the midst of a set of immense large drawing rooms. The first glance I got into one of these large drawing rooms, I got a terrible start, thinking I had seen my brother William — whereas it was myself.'

During James' sojourn in London the cholera epidemic was raging. He mentions in the following correspondence, dated February 5, 1832, that the account he has heard regarding Scotland is dreadful and warns Margaret to be sure and allow no beggars to approach the house, convinced that they are the culprits, guilty of spreading the infection over the whole country. So grave is his concern that he informs her of his intention to write to Dr Russel, requesting him to set guards at the public's expense, to prevent vagrants from entering the parish.

Margaret's reply is 'newsy' to say the least, telling in detail of everything that is happening in the neighbourhood and also giving her husband a gentle chiding. 'You have really had a grand Festival, but I should have wished you kept your seat, what in all the world took you upon the top of the table? I have some small hopes that the papers have been quizzing, your speech was an extraordinary one.

'The children are wearying greatly for you. I cannot tell which of them speaks most about you. Jas says he gets sick for want of you, poor fellow he misses you much he has nobody to make sport with him. Hetty would be glad to see you and dear little Mary Gray is much improved, she is a sweet good baby. Now be sure and write immediately. The children send kisses and we hope soon to see you,' she closes, obviously wanting him home.

Finally, in March Altrive is treated to some surprising enlightenment. 'I got a public dinner from the great Walton-Cotton club yesterday, was made an honorary member and decorated with the order. You must consult your own heart whether you would like to be Lady Hogg, or remain the Ettrick Shepherdess, because you may now have the former title if you please. The Queen, is it seems, intent on it and I got a letter the other day from Lord Montague, requesting me not to see His Majesty until he and I consulted together, as he understood there was some risk of being knighted, which would run me into the expense of at least £300 of fees. For my part, I despise it in our present circumstances and could see no good that it could do to us. It might indeed introduce our family into the first ranks, but then where is £300, to come from? In short, I want you to dissuade me from it, but I'll not look near His Majesty till I hear from you, so write me directly. Dr Brewster was knighted yesterday.

'The cholera, is raging and spreading terribly here now, but do not say a word about that to James, else it will kill him.

'How I am longing to have you all, one by one, in my arms again. Bestow a benediction on every one of our dear, dear, children in their father's name and kiss each of them for me.'

'Your affectionate husband James Hogg. '

To Jas Hogg Esq,
11, Waterloo Place,
London.
Altrive Lake, March 15th. 1832.

My ever dearest James,

From my heart, I can say I like no such titles and if you value your own comfort and my peace of mind, you will at once, if offered to you, refuse it. It is an honour you may be proud to refuse, but not to accept. I think a title to a poor man, is a load scarcely bearable.

I daresay there are many men born with one on their back, who would be thankful if they could to get rid of it. Her Majesty must be entirely ignorant of your circumstances — if the thing has ever really been thought of — so I hope if you are to have an interview with their Majesties, you will in your own short pithy way, express your gratitude for the honour they intended to confer upon you, assuring them you know they wish you well, but from prudent reasons, you must decline the offer.

Did I possess five thousand a year, I should wish to be unencumbered with a title. I want no more than to be the wife of plain James Hogg. We ought to consult the happiness of our family and such a thing I should look upon in every respect, would be to them in all probability, great misery. I could say a thousand against it, did I consider it at all necessary, but not doubting for a moment your seeing the impropriety of it, shall say little more, only I must say, should you come back with such a burden on your shoulders, you will return infinitely poorer than when you left me, suppose you were to add hundreds to your income.

Thank God we are all well except Jas who has been

complaining for some time. He is seldom two days well at one time, yet he is better than he has been and I flatter myself when you return he will get quite well. He is very tall and looks rather delicate. He has not been at school for a month, of course has made little progress in his learning since you left. He gets lessons at home but is not as hearty in the cause as we would wish. Dear Little Mary was inoculated on Saturday and appears to be doing well. Mr Anderson I expect back at the end of the week to see her. All the children and myself are wearying terribly for you to come back. Do, I beseech you, come immediately. You have already been three months away from us. Should you be at the Palace take good notice for I should like to hear about our good King and Queen and consult Lord Montague or some other prudent friend as to your dress. I should wish you to appear as plain as possible, to be consistent with the place.

I have settled so far a number of little accounts. All unasked for and am trying to get the house forward, the wood is got and the passage is to be opened up very soon. Come in the end of the month, really I feel great anxiety about you at this time. May God be with you and preserve you in health. I think you had better come by land though it is more expensive. I see by the newspapers, cholera has been in some of the London packets. Write before you leave London — if you come by Selkirk, I shall get a gig and send to meet you. As I hope to see you soon I shall finish this letter.

Your ever affect, M. Hogg

My dear Papa

I have not been well since you left us but I think I shall get well when you come home now dear Papa come this month — your affect. son Jas Hogg.

11 Waterloo Place, March 23rd. 1832

My beloved Margt,

Your last has fairly upset my resolution of remaining here any longer, my dear boy's health being far dearer to me than either honour or riches, of course I shall neither see the King nor Queen. I called on the Duke of Buccleuch yesterday, but find that he will not arrive here before the 28th., so I shall not see him either, but I will call again on Sir Montague. I dine again with the Highland Society tonight and shall meet with many of the first nobles of the land, this being their great anniversary. I leave London tomorrow evening and sail for Edinburgh on Sabbath morning in the United Kingdom steamship, which never takes above fifty two hours at farthest in a trip, so that I shall be in Edinburgh in all probability on Tuesday the 27th., where at Mr Watson's, I shall be happy to meet with you and Mary and Harriet, or if you cannot possibly get away, you might send Peggy with her. I will buy her a new hat or anything she needs there. If you do not meet me I will make as little stay in Edinburgh as possible, but haste home. I am positively worried with kindness so that I do not know what to do first and I positively will not come to London again without you. I am in excellent good health and

Your ever affectionate husband, James Hogg

On his return to Scotland, James attended yet another congratulatory dinner at Peebles, presided over by his old friend John Wilson.

Replying to the toast, he said that he had sought fame in both the mountains and the city, but only now, on seeing so many notable men gathered together on his account, did he feel that he had found her.

Following his London visit, James was never quite so vigorous again, displaying repeated bouts of illness which prevented him going to both church and market. Lockhart, when he beheld him, described his friend as appearing 'wet, weary and unwell'.

A short while later, Cochrane, James' new publisher, became bankrupt. Only a single volume of the *Altrive Tales* which was to start the collected edition was published.

During the following two years no new manuscripts were printed. In 1834, however, he produced a series of lay sermons, which were keenly accepted and that same year *The Domestic Manners and Private Life of Sir Walter Scott*, the 'indelicacies' of which cost him his friendship with Lockhart.

Although peace was achieved with Blackwood, their friendship never resumed. Blackwood, by then an old man, died in 1834.

Over the years, Altrive was added to and improved upon. In August, 1833, a Mrs Grant of Laggan described it thus: 'Altrive is just such a place as you fancy for the abode of a gentle shepherd; the house quite comfortable, looking better than you would expect — sheltered by a few tall trees and standing on a most pastoral, indeed, a very pretty knowe, with a very extensive view; a comely crop, beginning to look yellow below and the Yarrow, nearly circling round it; a useful garden, not without flowers, nor wholly without

weed and rather more thistles blooming on the brae than
you would have tolerated. But the shepherd has little of that
''retired leisure, that in trim gardens takes its pleasure''.
Consequently, the place looks as though it has been made
on purpose for him.'

In the month of July, James surprised his son with an
invitation to ride with him to Blackhouse, on the Douglas
burn, where the shepherd's first advent of genius dawned.
Following this excursion, on the 'Glorious Twelfth', for he
would not miss the occasion as long as he was able to fire a
gun, he asked young James to accompany him along the
heights of Riskenhope, so that he could look once more on
Ettrick Water and view the lonely cottage that was his
birthplace. He remained there in silence for 30 minutes,
seated on the hillside.

Soon afterwards, he was taken ill with jaundice (the
shepherd's bane) and by November was confined to his
bed. Friends too numerous to mention visited the house.

On the seventeenth of November he became speechless.
Sandy Laidlaw came down from Bowerhope each day and
towards the end remained permanently in the room. Mrs
Richardson, better known as Tibbie Shiel, who had been in
service for a number of years with James' mother, stayed
by him to the last and it was she who closed his eyes.

John Wilson arrived just too late. James died on
November 21, 1835. 'Often I saw him, an uncomplaining
sufferer, as he lay on a bed of sickness, when the hand of
death had touched him. I came again but it was to visit the
fatherless and widow in their affliction, for the silver cord
had just been loosed, and the golden bowl broken.

'In a few days more they bore him to the quiet church
yard of Ettrick, near to the spot where he had first drawn

breath and laid him in the place of his father's sepulchres. Many a sorrowing friend was there, many a shepherd in his grey plaid; and one was there, beside his only son, who might be called the chief mourner, for he loved him with the affection of a brother.'

Who that was present could forget the noble form of John Wilson — a model for a sculptor — as he stood at the top of the grave, his cloak wrapped around him, his head uncovered, his long auburn hair streaming in the wind, while tears flowed down his manly countenance. Absorbed in his own sad and solemn meditations, with difficulty he tore himself away from the dust of one so dear to him.

Friends raised 'a good sum' for Margaret and her young family. The money was put into a trust to provide them with an income. For a few winters she went with the children to Edinburgh where they were being educated, eventually going to reside there permanently.

The Duke of Buccleuch benevolently arranged an annuity in lieu of the farm and there were small amounts coming in from Blackie's edition of her husband's works. After being widowed for 18 years Margaret was eventually granted a pension from the Civil List.

All men who have turned out worth anything have had the chief hand in their own education.
                                    Sir Walter Scott. June, 1830.

Sir Walter Scott

10
SIR WALTER SCOTT
1771 - 1832

At the end of *The Heart of Midlothian* Sir Walter describes
the original of Madge Wildfire as a wandering shepherdess
called 'Feckless Fanny', who drove a small flock about the
countryside.

'She had for each a different name, to which it answered
when it was called by its mistress and would likewise obey
in the most surprising manner any command she thought
proper to give. When she lay down in the fields at night, for
she would never enter a house, they always disputed who
should lie next to her, by which means she was kept warm,
while she lay in the midst of them; when she attempted to
rise from the ground, an old ram whose name was Charlie,
always claimed the sole right of assisting her; pushing any
that stood in his way aside, until he arrived right before his
mistress; he then bowed his head nearly to the ground so
that she might lay her hands on his horns, which were very
large; he then raised her gently from the ground by raising
his head. If she chanced to leave her flock feeding, as soon
as they discovered she had gone, they all began to bleat
most piteously and would continue to do so until she
returned; they would then testify their joy by rubbing their
sides against her petticoat and frisking about.'

One day, while passing through Moffat Charlie broke
into a kale patch and was worried to death by the owner's
mastiff. This terrible deed almost broke Fanny's heart and

she would not leave the side of her beloved ram for several days. It was with much difficulty that she consented to allow him to be buried. The ram's grave, which she visited each year, is called, 'The Leddy's Know' and Sir Walter maintained that the Moffat school boys, held it sacred in his day.

James Hogg describes an excursion to Moffat in the harmonious company of Sir Walter, Willie Laidlaw the Abbotsford factor and Sir Adam Ferguson: 'I conducted them through that wild region, by a path which if not rode by Clavers, was I dare say, never rode by another gentleman. Sir Adam rode into a gulph inadvertantly and got a sad fright, but Scott in the very worse paths never dismounted, save at Loch Skene to take some dinner. We went to Moffat that night, where we met with some of his family — and such a day and night of glee I never witnessed. Our perils were matter to him of infinite merriment; and there was a short-tempered boot boy at the inn, who wanted to pick a quarrel with him, at which he laughed till the water ran over his cheeks. I was disappointed in never seeing some incident in his sub-sequent works laid in a scene resembling the rugged solitudes around Loch Skene, for I never saw him survey any scene with so much attention. A single serious look at the scene, generally filled his mind with it and he seldom took another; but here he took all the names of all the hills and their altitudes and relative situations with regard to one another and made me repeat them several times.'

Sir Walter Scott was born August 15, 1771, in College Wynde, Edinburgh, one of 13 children, the first six of whom died in infancy. His father, also Walter Scott, was a solicitor and Writer to the Signet. His mother Anne

Rutherford, was the daughter of Dr J. Rutherford MD, also of Edinburgh.

At the tender age of 18 months, baby Walter was struck down by a serious illness which was to leave him lame for the rest of his life. Until the age of eight he lived at his grandfather's farm at Sandyknowe, near Smailholme, where he became a firm favourite of the shepherd, auld Sandy Ormiston, 'near whom he was laid down out of doors and soon began, through mere childish impatience, to stand, to walk and to run'. It was Sandy who through time instilled in Walter's youthful mind all the lore of the countryside. On numerous occasions the young ewe-milkers would carry the child on their backs and were amazed at how quickly he 'kenned every sheep and lamb by the marks on their heads'.

After leaving Sandyknowe Walter lived with an uncle at Kelso. From then until his marriage in 1797 he lived with his parents. He was educated at the High School and, after studying law at the University of Edinburgh, he became an advocate.

In 1797 on Christmas Eve Walter Scott married Margaret Charlotte Charpentier, the daughter of M. Jean Charpentier of Lyons, France, at Carlisle.

The couple lived partly in Edinburgh and partly at Lasswade Cottage. In 1802 they bought 39 Castle Street. This was their Edinburgh house until 1826, when it was sold as a result of Sir Walter's financial crash. In 1799 Sir Walter was made sheriff-depute of Selkirkshire, which necessitated a house nearer his work. In 1804, they made the move to Ashiestiel, beside the Tweed, several miles from the eventual Abbotsford. His new employment gave him ample time to carry on his writing and various other activities so far denied him. He was a skilled horseman and became a cavalryman in the Volunteers, on one occasion riding 100 miles in a day when an invasion by the French was rumoured.

Sir Walter and his wife Charlotte had four children, two boys and two girls. The elder son, also Walter — afterwards the second baronet — was to eventually command the 15th Hussars at Bangalore. He died tragically at sea in 1847 off the Cape of Good Hope. Charles, the younger son, joined the diplomatic service. He died in Teheran in 1841. Anne, the younger daughter, survived her father by only a year. Sophia, the eldest, married John Gibson Lockhart in 1820. Today he is best remembered as a biographer of his father-in-law. Educated at Glasgow University and Balliol College, Oxford, he became editor of *The Quarterly Review* from 1825 until a year before his death in 1854.

Sophia bore him three children: John Hugh, known as Hugh Littlejohn, for whom Sir Walter wrote *The Tales of a Grandfather*, died when only 10; Walter Lockhart Scott, who succeeded to Abbotsford but died unmarried at Versailles in 1853 and Charlotte who married James Robert Hope QC in 1847.

On the death of her brother Charlotte took on the inheritance, both she and her husband taking the additional surname of Scott. They also had three children, two of whom died in infancy. The third, Mary Monica, at the time of her marriage in 1874, was not only the grand-daughter of Sir Walter Scott, but was also his only surviving descendant.

Mary Monica and her husband, the Hon. Joseph Constable Maxwell, third son of William, tenth Baron Herries, of Everingham Park, York, and of Caerlaverock Castle, Dumfriesshire, produced eight children and also added the name of Scott to their surname, the eldest son,

Walter Maxwell-Scott, eventually succeeded to the property. His two daughters, Patricia Maxwell-Scott and Dame Jean, who is Lady-in-Waiting to Princess Alice, survive him.

Abbotsford, situated close to the historic town of Melrose, is undoubtedly a happy house, exhibiting a gentle aura of peace and tranquility. Sir Walter's benevolent presence, as well as his deep affection for his home, is felt everywhere but especially in his study. It takes little in the way of imagination to envisage him hard at work, surrounded by his beloved books and dogs, seated at his writing desk, a copy of one he greatly admired belonging to John Morrit of Rokeby in Yorkshire, who often provided him with a place to stay when he journeyed to and from London by coach.

In 1935 an exciting discovery was made when the desk was found to conceal two secret drawers, one of which contained 57 letters written by Sir Walter to his wife both before and after their marriage. These letters were edited by Sir Herbert Grierson in 1937, (Vol XII, London) and published in *The Letters of Sir Walter Scott*. When Charlotte died in 1826 Sir Walter wrote in his journal that his heart must break.

I made my first acquaintance with Abbotsford when I visited the house in 1985 with my aunt, a Sister with the Church of England. We were treated with such warmth and kindness that I was determined to return. Two years later, I received a telephone call from Dame Jean Maxwell-Scott, who is a great-great-great grand-daughter of Sir Walter. Miss Jean, as she is affectionately known, asked for copies of both my books and invited Geoff and I to visit her. We were of course, delighted to accept the invitation.

Abbotsford

On arrival we were shown various family portraits in the private apartments. A watercolour that nostalgically stands out in my memory is that of a shepherd seated on a hillside, watched by a small boy, both of whom are dressed in the attire of a former century.

The gardens especially caught and held our attention. To say that the colours were impressive is putting it mildly. The delightful blend of pastel against vivid and unusual shades, coupled with exquisite birdsong, sunshine and shadow, made the experience one we would never forget.

We were introduced, first of all, to the gardeners then taken to the tearoom for refreshment, served by cordial ladies who showed great interest in our lifestyles as shepherds and in our dogs. Finally, after promising to bring along our canine friends when next we paid them a visit, we said goodbye.

The original Abbotsford had been bought by Sir Walter in 1811 from the Rev. Dr Robert Douglas of Galashiels for £4000. It is described by Lockhart as consisting of a rich haugh along the banks of the Tweed, with around 100 acres of undulating ground behind; all of which was undrained, badly enclosed and much of it covered by nothing better than the native heath. The farmhouse itself was poor looking, with a kale yard on one flank and a staring barn, erected by the previous owner, on the other. In front there was a filthy pond covered with ducks and duckweed! It is therefore not surprising that the whole area was known as 'Clarty Hole' rather than by the correct name of Cartley-hole. Within an hour of taking possession, Sir Walter had renamed the farm Abbotsford after an adjoining ford situated just below the house that in earlier times had belonged to the monks of the great abbey of Melrose.

Sir Walter had visited the area in his boyhood. His

imagination was fired by the historical connections of the region, as well as the intrigue of the river and surrounding countryside and he nurtured a lasting desire to return. It was his father who had suggested that they alight from the carriage 'and see a thing quite in your line'. They walked together to a round stone half a mile above the Tweed that commemorates the place

> *Where gallant Cessford's life-blood dear*
> *Reeked on dark Elliot's border spear.*

'Here at Turn-again, close by the House of Scott, ended the savage pursuit of Buccleuch's men in 1526, after the Battle of Melrose. From this famous vantage point overlooking the river one was within easy reach of Melrose Abbey, the ruined tower of Darnick, the Catrail, Cauldshiels Loch — the rumoured locality where Thomas the Rhymer finally disappeared from the sight of men — and the eventual site of Abbotsford.

'For more than a month my head was fairly tenanted by ideas, which, though strictly pastoral and rural, were neither literary nor poetical. Long sheep and short sheep and tups and gimmers and hoggs and dinmonts had made a perfect sheep-fold of my understanding.' Sir Walter was apologising for not replying to a letter when preparing for the flit from their 'Sweet little cottage on the banks of the Esk' (at Lasswade).

'Owing to the death of Colonel Russell, the heir being in India, a tenancy had become vacant at Ashestiel and the small farm adjoining. The family was to spend several contented and happy years here, before moving six miles downstream to take up residence at Abbotsford.'

On the death of his uncle, Captain Robert Scott of Kelso, Sir Walter came into possession of Rosebank Cottage 'and about thirty acres of the finest land in Scotland. It is expected to sell to a great advantage. I shall buy a mountain farm with the purchase money and be quite the Laird of the Cairn and Scaur,' Sir Walter enthused. Rosebank eventually sold for £5000. Lockhart noted that 'this good fortune made an important change in his pecuniary position and influenced accordingly the arrangements of his future life. Independent of practice at the Bar and of literary profits, he was now in possession of a fixed revenue of nearly, if not quite, £1000 a year'.

He engaged Tom Purdie, whom he had met in his capacity as sheriff on a charge of poaching, as 'general factotum'. Apart for his fondness for 'the dram', Tom proved a satisfactory choice. However, there was cause for Sir Walter to threaten him on more than one occasion with the epitaph: 'Here lies one who might have been entrusted with untold gold, but not with unmeasured whisky.'

Peter Mathieson was employed as coachman in that same year of 1804 and, by all accounts, not before time. His wife, for one, had until then endured some narrow escapes in the phaeton when her husband took the reins!

From my research the boldest spiders fled,
And moths retreating trembled, as I read.

                                              Sir Walter Scott.

Whilst in residence at Ashestiel Lockhart wrote of the household's busy life-style: 'He, (Sir Walter) rose by five o'clock, lit his own fire when the season required one and shaved and dressed with great deliberation — for he was a very martinet as to all but the mere coxcomberies of the toilet, not abhorring effeminate dandyism itself so cordially as the slightest approach to personal slovenliness, or even those "bed-gown and slippers tricks", as he called them, in which literary men are so apt to indulge. Arrayed in his shooting-jacket, or whatever dress he meant to use till dinner time, he was seated at his desk by six o'clock, all his papers arranged before him in the most accurate order and his books of reference marshalled around him on the floor, while at least one favourite dog lay watching his eye, just beyond the line of circumvallation. Thus by the time the family assembled for breakfast between nine and ten, he had done enough (in his own language) "to break the neck of the day's work".

'After breakfast, a couple of hours more were given to his solitary tasks and by noon, he was, as he used to say, "his own man". When the weather was bad he would labour incessantly all morning; but the general rule was to be out and on horseback by one o'clock at the latest; while, if any more distant excursion had been proposed overnight, he was ready to start on it by ten; his occasional working days of unintermitted study forming, as he said, a fund in his favour, out of which he was entitled to draw for accommodation whenever the sun shone with special brightness.'

Visitors flocked in and out of Ashestiel. Friends came and stayed for weeks at a time. Whereas some were undoubtedly welcome, others arrived purely out of curiosity. To occupy all of these callers took a great deal of patience and ingenuity. At the same time Sir Walter was engaged in legal duties in Edinburgh and in the Sheriff Court in Selkirk. He was also partnering Ballantynes in printing and publishing, as well as keeping an eye on manuscripts submitted to them. He was undoubtedly a man of great physical energy and exceptional determination, his sense of humour and ability to switch off keeping him going when all else failed. The Ettrick Shepherd was heard to comment 'the more mischief, the better sport for him'.

The Lay of The Last Minstrel, Marmion, The Lady of The Lake and part of *Waverley* are some of the great works composed by the bard at Ashestiel, the labour of his pen bringing him rich rewards, while his fame as a writer spread. Under such circumstances it came as no surprise that along with the sweetness of success, Sir Walter tasted the bitterness of envy. I wonder at his feelings on receiving the following advice from Leigh Hunt:

Be original man; study more, scribble less;
Nor' mistake present favours for lasting success;
And remember if laurels are what you would find,
The crown of all triumph is freedom of mind.

In a letter to James Ballantyne dated 1811, Sir Walter wrote: 'My lease to Ashestiel is out — I now sit a tenant at will under a heavy rent and at all the inconvenience of one when in the house of another. I have therefore resolved to purchase a piece of land sufficient for a cottage and a few fields... They stretch along the Tweed, near halfway between Melrose and Selkirk... I have serious thoughts of one or both and must have recourse to my pen to make the matter easy... It is proper, John, that you should be as soon as possible apprised of these my intentions, which I believe you will think reasonable in my situation and at my age, while I may yet hope to sit under a tree of my own planting.'

Of the £4000 that he paid for Abbotsford, Sir Walter received half from his brother, Major John Scott, while the

Ballantynes obliged by advancing the remainder, using the as yet unwritten *Rokeby* as security.

The Scotts, along with their children, Sophia, Walter, Anne and baby Charles, finally moved from Ashestiel to Abbotsford at the May term in 1812. In regard to this upheaval Sir Walter mused: 'The neighbours have been much delighted with the procession of my furniture, in which old swords, bows, targets and lances made a very conspicuous show. A family of turkeys was accommodated within the helmet of some preux chevalier of ancient Border fame; and the very cows, for ought I know, were bearing banners and muskets. I assure your ladyship that this caravan, attended by a dozen ragged, rosy, peasant children, carrying fishing rods and spears and leading ponies, greyhounds and spaniels, would, as it crossed the Tweed, have furnished no bad subject for the pencil and really reminded me of one of the gipsy groups of "Callot" upon their march.'

Sir Walter described Abbotsford as looking charming. 'As for the house and the poem (*Rokeby*), there are twelve masons hammering at the one and one poor noddle at the other.'

An old bed curtain was nailed up across the room close behind his chair and there, whenever the spade, the dibble, or the chisel were laid aside, he pursued his poetical tasks, apparently undisturbed and unannoyed by the surrounding confusion of masons and carpenters, to say nothing of the ladies' small talk, the children's babble among themselves, or their repetition of their lessons.

Sir Walter was a doting father who brought his children up in the belief that 'without courage there cannot be truth and without truth there can be no other virtue'.

Rokeby, *The Bridal of Triermain*, followed in 1814 by *Waverley*, the second and third volumes of which were completed in the short space of three weeks, all these helped increase his income by a considerable amount.

The following year, *Guy Mannering* became an instant success. Two thousand copies at a guinea each were sold the day after publication.

Sir Walter's increasing rise in fame and circumstance encouraged him to fulfil a longstanding ambition in the purchase of more land. Both Kaeside and Toftfield (later to be renamed Huntly Burn) were added to Abbotsford in 1817.

He was now master of all these haunts of True Thomas and of the whole ground of the Battle of Melrose, from Skirmish-field to Turn-again. His enjoyment of the new territory was, however, interrupted by various returns of the cramp and the depression of spirit, which always attended, in his case, the use of opium — the only medicine that seemed to have power over the disease. It was while struggling with such languor on one lovely evening in the autumn of 1817 that he wrote the following beautiful verses. They mark the very spot of their birth — namely, the then naked height overhanging the northern side of the Cauldshiels Loch, from which Melrose Abbey to the east and the hills of Ettrick and Yarrow to the west are now visible over a wide range of woodland, all the work of the poet's hand.

The sun upon the Weirdlaw Hill,
In Ettrick's vale is sinking sweet;
The westland wind is hush and still —
The lake lies sleeping at my feet.
Yet not the landscape to mine eye
Bears those bright hues that once it bore;
Though evening with her richest dye,
Flames o'er the hills of Ettrick's shore.

With listless look along the plain
I see Tweed's silver current glide,
And coldly mark the holy fane
Of Melrose ride in ruined pride.
The quiet lake, the balmy air,
The hill, the stream, the tower, the tree —
Are they still such as once they were,
Or is the dreary change in me?

Thus wrote, I suspect, a weary of spirit bard, rather than a disillusioned man. Sir Walter undoubtedly worked like a Trojan in order to enjoy his estate, his family and his many friends.

Summer afternoons were spent picnicking on the banks of Cauldshiels Loch, evenings were spent reading out loud after dining on forest mutton and during the day guests were treated to guided tours of the area — favourite haunts being the historic town of Melrose and scenic Yarrow.

In between times, there were bushels of acorns to be sown and thousands of trees to be planted. The acorns arrived by both land and sea; friends of Sir Walter gathered them in Windsor Forest until their backs ached. The Earl of Fife sent seed of Norway pine. Lord Montague sent lime. Sir Walter himself ordered 3000 elms, 3000 horse chestnuts and the same quantity of laburnums, 2000 sweet briars and 100,000 of his favourite birches. (On an amusing note, I happened to mention to Patricia Maxwell-Scott how impressed I was with the amount of planting Sir Walter accomplished, explaining how exhausted my husband appeared after planting only 1000 trees. With a smile, she was quick to reassure me that Sir Walter had been given assistance.)

There were acres of grass to be mown, the haugh was to

be ploughed and there was mortar to mix. He had Clerk of Session duties to attend to in Edinburgh as well as his work in Selkirk as Sheriff of the county, and during all of these activities he still found time to be involved in the firm of Ballantyne.

Washington Irvine recorded his visit in 1817, when the walls of the new Abbotsford were already higher in proportion than the original cottage. 'The noise of my chaise had disturbed the quiet of the establishment. Out sallied the warder of the castle, a black greyhound and leaping on one of the blocks of stone began a furious barking. The alarm brought out the whole garrison of dogs, all open-mouthed and vociferous. In a little while, the lord of the castle himself made his appearance. I knew him at once, by the likeness that had been published of him. He came limping up the gravel walk, aiding himself by a stout walking staff. By his side jogged along a large iron-grey staghound, of most grave demeanour.'

After a second breakfast and an excursion into Melrose escorted by Charles, Sir Walter's youngest child, Irving was accompanied on a ramble.

'Our ramble took us on the hills commanding an extensive prospect. "Now," said Scott, "I have brought you, like the pilgrim in the Pilgrim's Progress, to the top of the Delectable Mountains, that I may show you all the goodly regions hereabouts. Yonder is Lammermuir and Smailholme; and there you have Galashiels and Torwoodlee and Gala Water; and in that direction you see Teviotdale and the Braes of Yarrow and Ettrick stream winding along like a silver thread, to throw itself into the Tweed".

'He went on thus to call over names celebrated in Scottish song, and most of which had recently received a romantic interest from his own pen. In fact I saw a great

part of the Border country spread out before me and could
trace the scenes of those poems and romances which had in
a manner bewitched the world.

'I gazed about me for a time with mute surprise, I may
almost say with disappointment. I beheld a mere succession
of grey waving hills, line upon line as far as the eye could
reach, monotonous in their aspect and so destitute of trees,
that one could almost see a stout fly walking along their
profile; and the far-famed Tweed appeared a naked stream
flowing between bare hills, without a tree or thicket on its
banks; and yet such had been the magic web of poetry and
romance thrown over the whole, that it had a greater charm
for me than the richest scenery I had beheld in England. I
could not help giving utterance to my thoughts. Scott
hummed for a moment to himself and looked grave; he had
no idea of having his muse complimented at the expense of
his native hills. "It may be pertinacity," said he at length;
"but to my eye, these grey hills and all this wild Border
country, have beauties peculiar to themselves. I like the
very nakedness of the land, it has something bold and stern
and solitary about it. When I have been for sometime in the
rich scenery about Edinburgh, which is like ornamented
garden land, I begin to wish myself back again among my
own honest grey hills; and if I did not see the heather, at
least once a year, I think I should die." The last words were
said with an honest warmth, accompanied by a thump on
the ground with his staff, by way of emphasis, that showed
his heart was in his speech. He vindicated the Tweed too, as
a beautiful stream in itself.

'The evening having passed away delightfully in a
quaint-looking apartment, half study, half drawing room,
Scott read several passages from the old *Romance of Arthur*
with a fine, deep, sonorous voice and a gravity of tone that

seemed to suit the antiquated black-letter volume.

'It was a rich treat to hear such a work read by such a person and in such a place; and his appearance, as he sat reading, in a large arm-chair, with his favourite hound Maida at his feet and surrounded by books and reliques and Border trophies, would have formed an admirable and most characteristic picture. When I retired for the night, I found it almost impossible to sleep: the idea of being under the roof of Scott; of being on the Borders on the Tweed, in the very centre of that region which had, for some time past, been the favourite scene of romantic fiction; and above all, the recollections of the ramble I had taken, the company in which I had taken it and the conversation which had passed, all fermented in my mind and nearly drove sleep from my pillow.'

In the autumn of 1818, although Abbotsford was still far from complete, Sir Walter decided to give a house-warming, or handselling, as he preferred to call it. Fifteen guests were invited to dinner, including Lockhart, who was seeing the house for the first time and afterwards described the occasion as 'the gayest' that he had attended. Once the potage a la Meg Merrilees had been devoured, John of Skye, who spent his days hedging and ditching on the estate, appeared at the window in full Highland regalia.

'When the cloth was drawn and the never failing salver of quaichs introduced, John of Skye, upon some well-known signal, entered the room, but en militaire without removing his bonnet and taking his station behind the landlord, received from his hand the largest of the Celtic bickers, brimful of Glenlivet. The man saluted the company in his own dialect, tipped off the contents at a gulp, wheeled about as solemnly as if the whole ceremony had been a movement on parade and forthwith, recommenced his pibrochs and gatherings.' Lockhart noted that Sir Walter had never appeared in such high spirits as he was that evening and never saw him in higher again. Abbotsford was considered by those present a marvellous building.

Once dinner was over, the guests were invited to the new western turret, in order to gaze on Tweed at its loveliest, shimmering by moonlight. Sir Walter promised: 'If I live, I will build me a higher tower, with a more spacious platform and a staircase better fitted for an old fellow's scrambling.' John of Skye was heard tuning his pipes below and Sir Walter called for *Lochaber no more*.

By the year 1820 the estate had been increased to around 1400 acres. It was at this time that Sir Walter was to gain his highest accolade. He journeyed by coach to London to receive his baronetcy. 'I shall always reflect with pleasure on Sir Walter Scott's having been the first creation of my reign,' said King George IV, when Sir Walter kissed his hand.

'Abbotsford is now considered the place to visit,' Lockhart imparted. 'It would hardly, I believe, be too much to affirm that Sir Walter Scott entertained under his roof, in the course of the seven or eight brilliant seasons when his prosperity was at its height, as many persons of distinction in rank, in politics, in art, in literature and in science, as the most princely nobleman of his age ever did in the like space of time... of the eminent foreigners who visited the island in this period, a moiety crossed the Channel mainly in consequence of the interest with which his writings had invested Scotland — and that the hope of beholding the man under his own roof was the crowning motive with half that moiety. As for countrymen of his own, like him enobled, in the higher sense of that word, by the display of intellectual energies, if any one such contemporary can be pointed out as having crossed the Tweed and yet not spent a day at Abbotford, I shall be surprised.'

In 1822 Sir Walter persuaded George IV to come to Scotland — the first reigning monarch to do so for 180 years. He induced him to restore the peerages withdrawn from Scots after the Jacobite Rebellion when Bonnie Prince Charlie, and before him his father, rebelled against London. Sir Walter was also responsible for the return of the historical cannon known as Mons Meg to Edinburgh Castle.

Unfortunately, there came a point in Sir Walter's life when things began to go tragically wrong. He became involved in the bankruptcy of his publishers. According to H.J.C. Grierson, 'the tragic error of Scott's life, was to play author and publisher in one'.

'The impression made on my mind is not that of a gambler fevered with a thirst for gold, but of one to whom came, as in a dream, fairy-gold wealth, which enabled him to gratify his manifold desires and charities, but which as is the way with such gifts, disappeared as suddenly as it came. If he had been intent on money for its own sake, he could easily have made more and kept it longer. In all Scott did, there was the same blend of practical and imaginative interest.'

Sir Walter's own journal, which he began in November 1825 and ended in the midst of a sentence on April 16, 1832, gives the impression of his own agitation and feelings, both of despair and hope, as well as his determination to repay twenty shillings in the pound, by the fruits of his pen.

The building of Abbotsford and the purchase of the land had cost him around £70,000. Had this expenditure been all he might have avoided disaster. Unfortunately, more than

£100,000 was owed to his creditors.

At the height of despair Sir Walter wrote: 'I find my dogs' paws on my knees. I hear them whining and seeking me everywhere. This is nonsense. Poor Will Laidlaw! Poor Tom Purdie... Lady Scott is incredulous and persists in cherishing hope where there is no ground for hope... I wrote six of my close pages yesterday, which is about twenty four pages in print... I wrote till two o'clock — indeed till I was almost nervous with correcting and scribbling. I then walked, or rather was dragged throught the snow by Tom Purdie... Indifferent night — very bilious, which may be want of exercise... Now the shock of the discovery is past and over, I am much better off on the whole... I am free of an hundred petty public duties... I sleep and eat and work as I was wont... Give me popularity and all my present difficulties shall be as a joke in four years.'

The sum total of what Sir Walter owed was £130,000. At the end of 23 months he had written off £40,000. This amount being approximately six shillings in the pound, for which his creditors passed him a vote of thanks. During the following five years Sir walter worked both night and day. In April 1831 he recorded in his journal of 'a distinct stroke of paralysis affecting both my nerves and speech'.

In May of that year Lockhart described him thus: 'All his garments hung loose about him; his countenance was thin and haggard and there was an obvious distortion in the muscles of one cheek. His look, however, was placid — his eye as bright as ever — perhaps brighter than it ever was in health; he smiled with the same affectionate gentleness and though at first it was not easy to understand everything he said, he spoke cheerfully and manfully.'

At the time of this latest illness he was endeavouring to

finish *Count Robert* and on completion of the work was to begin writing *Castle Dangerous.*

It was decided that a recuperative sea voyage was in order. Two days before their departure for Italy William Wordsworth paid an unexpected visit to Abbotsford which cheered Sir Walter no end.

Before leaving careful instructions were imparted to William Laidlaw, the final paragraph of which repeated: 'To be very careful of the dogs.'

The trip to Naples was unsuccessful. Sir Walter yearned constantly for home. He eventually reached Newhaven on July 9, 1832, and was slung ashore in an unconscious state. Two days later, when he had regained a little of his strength, the journey to Abbotsford was undertaken.

'As we descended the vale of the Gala he began to gaze about him and by degrees it was obvious that he was recognizing the features of that familiar landscape. Presently, he murmured a word or two — ''Gala Water. Surely Buckholm, Torwoodlee.'' As we rounded the hill at Ladhope and the outline of the Eildons burst upon him, he became greatly excited and when turning himself on the couch his eye caught at length his own towers, at the distance of a mile, he sprang up with a cry of delight. The river being in flood, we had to go round a few miles by Melrose Bridge and during the time this occupied, his woods and home being within prospect, it required occasionally both Dr Watson's strength and mine (Lockhart) in addition to Nicolson's, to keep him in the carriage.

'After passing the bridge, the road for a couple of miles loses sight of Abbotsford and he relapsed into his stupor; but on gaining the bank immediately above it, his excitement became again ungovernable.

'Mr Laidlaw was waiting at the porch and assisted us in,

lifting him into the dining room, where his bed had been prepared. He sat bewildered for a few moments and then, resting his eye on Laidlaw said, "Ha! Willie Laidlaw! O man, how often I have thought of you."

'By this time his dogs had assembled about his chair — they began to fawn upon him and lick his hands and he alternately sobbed and smiled over them until sleep oppressed him.

'Sir Walter improved slightly the following day and was carried out into the garden. He sat quietly in the autumn sunshine, content in the company of both his grandchildren and his beloved dogs. He alternately admired the fruits of his labour — his garden, the trees he had planted with his own hands and the house that he had helped build. He began to believe that he might disappoint the doctors after all. He asked to be wheeled through his rooms. For an hour or so they wheeled him up and down the hall and in the library. "I have seen much," he said, "but nothing like my ain house. Give me one turn more!"

'A week later, he felt well enough to fling the plaids from off his shoulders, exclaiming, "This is sad idleness, I shall forget what I have been thinking of, if I don't get it down now. Take me into my own room and fetch the keys of my desk". His daughters got out his pens and he was wheeled into position. "Now give me my pen and leave me for a little to myself." Sophia, placed the pen in his fingers. He tried unsuccessfully to close them but his strength failed at the last moment and the pen dropped onto the paper. He lay back into his pillows, silent tears rolling down his cheeks.

'About half-past one p.m. on the 21st September, Sir Walter breathed his last in the presence of all his children. It was a beautiful day — so warm, that every window was wide open — and so perfectly still that the sound of all others most delicious to his ear, the gentle ripple of the Tweed over its pebbles, was distinctly audible as we knelt around the bed and his eldest son kissed and closed his eyes.'

On the way to his final resting place in Dryburgh Abbey the carriage horses paused out of habit at the place known as 'Scott's View'. They were allowed to stand for half an hour before continuing on their journey.

In the years that followed a constant stream of callers made a pilgrimage to Abbotsford. In 1883 there were 1500 visitors to the house, 20 of whom were from the United States.

On the August 22, 1886, Queen Victoria visited and took tea with the family. King George V and Queen Mary and the Duke and Duchess of York (later King George VI and Queen Elizabeth) came on July 23, 1923. The Duke and Duchess of Gloucester stayed for tea on August 26, 1964.

Although Sir Walter passed away at the relatively young age of 61 years, Abbotsford remains, an aesthetic reminder of his probity. All of his debts were cleared within a few years of his death.

Finally, one could not say goodbye to Abbotsford without mention of Maida, Sir Walter's favourite dog, with whom he shared a genuine understanding. To the right of the main door is a mounting block where Maida often sat. On top of this is a stone effigy of the much adored deerhound sculpted from life by John Smith in 1824. Maida, who died in the same year, lies buried beneath. The inscription is in Latin, Sir Walter translated thus:

Beneath the sculptured form which late you wore,
Sleep soundly Maida, at your master's door.

11
ENTERPRIZE CHALLENGE

Had I not been bubbling over with verve and enthusiasm regarding our venture into tourism and farming, I suppose it would have been easy to dub the mild winter of 1988/89 'a winter of discontent', for with a rise in interest and mortgage rates, there came an added vulnerability.

However, towards the latter part of November 1988, following a hectic, second season, what could well be described as a little bit of excitement crept into our lives in the shape of a lucrative business competition.

'The Enterprize Challenge', organised by the trustees of Cumbria and South Scotland Enterprize Trust, were endeavouring to encourage new business starts and small business development, with awards going to entrants who in the opinion of the panel of judges submitted the best proposals for the development of their business. The judges were to take into account the following criteria:

a. The originality of the business idea;

b. The financial viability of the entrant;

c. The potential of the business venture to generate additional employment.

Because there was £100,000 on offer in prize money we immediately submitted an entry and were subsequently delighted to learn that we had been chosen to participate in the semi-final, which was to be screened early in the new year by Border Television.

Compared with most of the other entrants our borrowing appeared high and we were not as yet in the position to provide full-time employment. Perhaps we should have put off entering until the following year? We debated; on the other hand our investment, namely the property, had doubled in value and we were desperately in need of capital for future development.

Before selection for the semi-final we were scrupulously vetted by the judges. They included an accountant, a successful businessman and a director of the Scottish Development Agency. All three paid us a visit shortly before Christmas. Our 'visitors' were greeted by us in 'the Bothy', as we now call the renovated shepherd's cottage. A cheery fire crackled in the old-fashioned range, recently black-leaded in readiness for the Yule-tide festivities. Various craft goods were on offer for inspection and by the window, coloured fairy-lights twinkled, adorning an enormous Christmas tree.

We were invited to divulge how we would spend the money were we fortunate enough to win. A tearoom within the Bothy; new kennelling for the dogs; a grandstand, so that visitors could view the demonstrations in comfort; picnic seats and tables... our list was endless.

As we contemplated beneath the home-made tinsel stars suspended from ancient smoke-blackened beams, I could not help but suppress a smile, momentarily comparing the adjudicators with the three wise men of Biblical times.

The other contestants in the semi-final were a shoe-maker, a photographer, a dressmaking duo, a forester and a graphic-designer, all of whom I was quick to note, appeared bright-eyed and bushy-tailed as we assembled beneath the television studio lights, while Geoff and I looked shattered, to say the least, after attending to our many animals before leaving home. We surmised that the all important decision had already been decided.

In my naivety and new rôle as a positive thinker, I admit
to being wildly enthusiastic — almost euphoric if I was
honest! This competition, I firmly believed, had been sent
purely to help us solve our present financial predicament.

It was time to announce the results. I squirmed excitedly
in my seat. In second place, the dressmaking duo who
manufactured up-market togs for youngsters down south.

There was a tie for first. I held my breath and crossed
both fingers and toes for added good luck. I might have
saved myself the bother. The announcement brought rapid
deflation when both the graphic-designer and the forester
romped past the post leaving us an also-ran. I rapidly
consoled myself with 'You win some, you lose some; no
good crying over spilled milk, etc.'.

Thankfully, we did not come away empty-handed. The
semi-finalists each received a monetary prize of £400
which, in our case, would go a long way towards providing
tearoom facilities, kennelling and picnic tables, when
matched with a grant from the Scottish Tourist Board. The
grandstand could easily be postponed for a little while
longer.

One month later, to our delight, we learned that we were to
be given a further prize of £1000 for rural diversification.
Following this surprise, an exciting invitation arrived
completely out of the blue, asking that we attend the Royal
Garden Party at Holyrood House.

There was however one small problem. My best hat, the
summery one adorned with pink ribbon and dried flowers
which I had proudly worn to the White House when visiting
the United States — the only suitable hat I owned for this
memorable occasion — had been nailed firmly to the wall
in the spare bedroom to cover up a damp patch.

During the long hot summer of 1989, Ross Ferguson, a young man from Peebles participating in an Employment Training Scheme run by the Borders Regional Council, practised the skill of dry-stane dyking at Tweedhopefoot and created a round sheep stell beside the burn below our cottage... and for the future, a breeding flock of black Welsh mountain ewes is being established.

Tweedhope Sheep Dogs, in three short years, has gone from being a wishful dream to becoming a reality.

Epilogue

Crouch House,
Harkstead.
February 7th. 1990.

Dear Geoff and Viv,

It's winter — that time of year when, weather permitting, most shepherds can plonk themselves in a comfy chair, kick off their taketty boots and put their feet up.

I realise that in your new role as 'entrepreneurs' you will be denied this luxury. You will both be preparing Tweedhopefoot for the onslaught of this year's visitors, making shepherds' crooks, training other people's dogs as well as your own and in your case Viv, finishing your latest book.

However, when you do have a quiet moment you will probably climb the steps to 'The Wee School' and sit down at one of the old desks in order to browse through some of the delightful comments written in the visitors' book. Line upon line of enthusiasms, put there by people who have travelled to see you and the dogs from all over the world — by coach, in cars and some like pilgrims, on foot. They have either read about what you are doing, or perhaps seen your dogs on television, or maybe they have heard a radio programme that sparked their interest. Sometimes their friends have recommended that they come and see for themselves and occasionally, as in my own case, it was simply serendipity.

I have visited Tweedhopefoot regularly over the past two years and on each occasion my stay has lasted twice as long as anticipated. Why you may wonder have I never added my comments in the visitors' book, particularly as I have spent so much time in your company? The reason is simple; I am unable to write all that I have to say on one line. You see, for me it has definitely been much more than 'Great', 'Wonderful', 'Marvellous' and 'Fantastic'. So by way of the following epilogue I would like to add my appreciation by describing what Tweedhopefoot has come to mean to me.

My Border collie Talla's conception coincided with another event, which although unrelated was to encourage me to buy a sheep dog. The effect of this decision has since completely changed my life.

Providence, destiny, fate — call it what you like — however one interprets the connecting principle which culminates in the 'special events' in one's life, I realise that discovering Tweedhopefoot was inevitable. Various seemingly unrelated circumstances had occurred in the months preceding my first visit, beginning with a preamble in Portugal. It was wintertime when my husband, Francois, and I were there. We had recently arranged to purchase Retorta, a small remote farm 15 kilometres across the lake from Santa Clara, in the hills of the Baix Alentejo — a poor and isolated region in the province north of the Algarve.

Our new neighbour, Inassio, is a shepherd. Like the other shepherds belonging to that area he does not use a dog to gather his sheep. Being over 70 years of age he relies on his son Antonio to care for the flock. Every morning Antonio takes the sheep to graze in the surrounding hills where they spend the day. As there are no walls or fences they are never left unattended for long and should they stray too far afield, Antonio whistles and calls them back to him by name. The leaders wear bells around their necks, and in the evening when the shadows lengthen and the lake is transformed into a vast shimmering vermilion, you can hear Antonio calling to his charges and the answering clang of the bells as the entire 'wealth of Inassio' wend their way homeward across the valley to a deserted homestead where they will be folded for the night. Only when 'all are safely gathered in', will Antonio climb the path to his own home, where already the lamps are alight, providing a welcoming glow.

Wild boars, although uncommon, live in these untamed hills, where rumours of wolves still abound. Nowadays, however, there is a more dangerous threat from 'incomers', who travel across the lake by boat, or arrive by four-wheel drive along the gravel roads — and worst of all, they are accompanied by their pet dogs, which they allow to race freely through the hills.

One day, just prior to Christmas, the worst happened. A dog chased and eventually killed one of Inassio's young ewes. We had planned to move to Portugal the following year and to take with us a dog; this unfortunate event set me wondering which breed of dog to take. A Border collie had to be the obvious choice because there were sheep all around us and we intended to have a flock of our own.

It was the New Year, a season of new beginnings. Far away, deep in the hills of the Scottish Border country, another shepherd unknown to me, was walking his dogs. He had noticed that his bitch Jan was in season and would soon be ready to be lined by Moss, a son of his wife's Laddie; and so begins the story of Talla — life for me would never be the same again!

Once we returned to England I spent the following months looking for a suitable pup. I had my heart set on a bitch. My search took me across Suffolk and included umpteen telephone calls. It was proving difficult to obtain a pup and very expensive to have a phone! Either one had not yet been born or else they had all been spoken for. Sometimes there were pups available but they were not bitches. I phoned a lady in Colchester who had 'a litter of eight ready to go' — they were all dogs! Then I rang a woman not far from where I lived. Hooray! She had two litters to choose from and plenty of bitches at £150 each! I swallowed hard, placed my cheque book in my pocket and raced over to 'pick a pup'. What I beheld on arrival appalled me. If this wasn't a 'puppy farm' then I don't know what is.

The place was filthy. I don't mean untidy, run-down or neglected, but filth like I had never seen before. This woman kept 40 collies in these conditions, in and around her semi-detached cottage. The garden had been turned into a muddy yard where the older dogs raced back and forth for exercise along a fence.

In the kitchen I was shown one litter, the other was in the living room. Between the two rooms, strolled any of the older dogs who wished to come in from outside. There was absolutely no protection against infection, even though the puppies were still young and vulnerable. A beautiful bitch pup, perfectly marked, with a full white collar was placed in my arms. She had a pair of matching blue eyes — that showed signs of infection. 'She's no good for showing. I'll knock £10 off because of her blue eyes,' persuaded the woman.

I realise that we can't all live in the environment that the Border collie prefers, but what we should do is examine our motives for keeping them. Feeling terribly sad for 'Blue Eyes' and her companions, I handed her back to her owner.

I left as quickly as possible, returning home with a heavy heart.

The following day, unbeknown to me, in a warm clean stable, Whitelaw Talla was born.

The telephone bill continued to soar! This time I was talking to a lady in Wiltshire — a friend of a friend of someone I had spoken to the previous day. She — surprise, surprise — didn't have any puppies either, but we got talking about dogs and sheep. I enquired if she knew of a place where a beginner could learn the art of handling and working a sheep dog. She informed me that there was such a place. It was called Tweedhopefoot and was run by a husband and wife, Geoff and Viv Billingham, who 'also writes books on the subject,' she added. 'And where might I find Tweedhopefoot?' I asked: 'Why in the Scottish Borders.' She replied, the tone of her voice implying 'where else?' This news sounded very encouraging — until then I'd felt it was very much a man's world I was entering. 'Apparently,' she continued, 'you can go there with your dog and be trained.' The place was sounding more and more promising. I remember thinking, 'isn't it amazing, how this particular phone call out of all the others, could make such a difference?'

So it was that I telephoned Viv first of all to obtain copies of her books and secondly to enquire about the possibility of visiting Tweedhopefoot as a student.

'Tweedsmuir 267,' sang the cheerful voice on the other end of the phone.

'I've been told that you train people as well as their dogs?' I enquired enthusiastically.

'Yes,' came the equally enthusiastic reply, 'but we haven't been here very long and there's an awful lot of developing to do.'

Then, like a whirlwind, she went on to describe in enraptured detail exactly what she and Geoff were trying to do and why. It all sounded wonderfully encouraging as well as practical and I was suitably impressed to enquire if when the time came, I could come along with my dog for some tuition.

'Do you have sheep?' asked Viv.

'Not at the moment, you see we are going to live in Portugal.' I went on to explain, 'and then we will get some, in the meantime I am looking for a puppy,' not for one minute expecting to hear, 'Oh! We've got a litter, what do you want, a little girl or a little boy?'

'A little girl,' I suppressed a giggle.

Viv giggled too calling out to her husband who was presumably in the same room, 'How many bitch pups are left?' Then back to me, 'It's my husband's bitch, he says there are two, one very black and smooth-coated like her mother, the other more flashy and longer-coated.'

'When can I come and see them?' I asked excitedly.

'Anytime,' came the reply. After saying goodbye I dashed off to find a road map.

Scotland? By heck it seems a long way... Tweedsmuir? Oh there it is. Wow! It's right in the middle of nowhere, great! Goodness, it's beside the River Tweed. I had no idea that the source was so far from the sea.

Come to think of it I had no idea about Scotland either, no idea about sheep and even less of an idea of how to work a sheep dog. Strangely I felt undaunted by my ignorance — sheer excitement and a sense of purpose was driving me on to I knew not where. It was a feeling I found to be irresistible.

Three weeks later my sister-in-law Estie and I drove to Scotland. Viv had sent the books as promised, along with a

delightful pen drawing of the puppy she thought would suit
me. She described her as 'a ball of fluff with an enormous
white star on her brow'. In fact the only reason she wasn't
keeping her herself was that she had a blue eye! The only
dog I had seen with a 'wall eye' was an old collie bitch that
worked cattle on a farm near Saxmundham in Suffolk. Her
owner, Wilf, proudly let me into a secret when I
commented on her odd eyes. 'Ah,' he said drily, 'the
shepherds say a blue eye be lucky, an' she bin right lucky
for me.'

At the time I did find it disconcerting looking at a dog
with odd coloured eyes, so I wasn't certain that the fluffy
pup would be the one I chose. However, I felt sure that on
this occasion I would be returning home with a pup. Viv
had said that if I didn't want one of theirs, she would help
me find another. In the meantime I had read *One Woman
and Her Dog* and enjoyed it. At that time the points on
training, handling and trialling meant nothing to me. It was
the story of Viv and Geoff's way of life that held me
spellbound - plus I wanted to meet Garry.

It's a strange feeling, but when you cross the Border
somewhere between Carlisle and Gretna Green, you
instinctively realise that you are in a different country —
and not just because the sign on the verge says 'Scotland'.
It feels, looks and smells different! For me the most striking
diversity is the dappled remoteness, from which one draws
a sense of awe as well as peace.

To be able to travel by car from Moffat to Edinburgh is
an experience not to be missed. The surrounding hills
remain as they have done since time immemorial. True
there is evidence of man's enterprise - skilfully built
drystane dykes snake the land, ruined farmsteads abound,

circular stells, ancient peels, hump-backed bridges as well as old inns, dot the landscape and perhaps more regrettably, acre upon acre of spruce. Yet still these hills retain strength, dignity and a sense of security.

This is Border country — sheep country; for me it has come to signify a boundary not only between the two countries, but the separation of two entirely different life-styles.

High above the Annan valley, Estie and I gazed on the bare loneliness of the Devil's Beeftub, then on through trees before descending to around 1100ft. Soon the road took us out of the forest and we observed stretching before us the valley along which the Tweed eagerly commences her path to the sea.

As we rounded a bend, there perched before us on a small hillock, at the foot of which babbled a burn, basked Tweedhopefoot in the warm glow of afternoon sunlight. Turning into the farm road we drove over a bridge and up the bank, stopping outside the farm buildings, where a bevy of joyful sheep dogs as well as their owners, were not slow to welcome us.

As we stepped from the car, I observed high in the cloudless sky, a hovering kestrel, symbol of freedom.

I will never forget the excitement I felt as I looked around me. It was as though a whole new chapter was starting in my life.

Viv introduced me to the dogs. First of all I met 'The Stars', then 'The Teenagers' and the 'Old Age Pensioners' — and finally, what we had travelled all this way to see, 'The Puppies'!

What is that indefinable 'something' that makes one choose a certain puppy? Jan had given birth to a litter of six healthy pups. Two were already sold — one having been exported to Dallas. Geoff had decided to keep 'Chocolate', a red and white dog pup, which he later named Roy. There, wriggling with happiness, were three pups to choose from. The smooth-coated brother and sister eagerly scrambled over each other in their race to reach my outstretched hand. Their fluffier sister had just woken up and placidly blinked her odd eyes at all the activity around her. She rose, yawned and stretched, before waddling over to see what all the fuss was about. What a little beauty she was — I immediately noticed that there was something 'special' about her. She was the one for me! As it turned out, my misgivings regarding living with a dog with different coloured eyes, were completely unfounded. When we returned home I easily deconditioned myself by wearing one earring, odd gloves, and odd socks, but drew the line at odd shoes!

The insistent clamourings of Drift, Maid, Nell, Nicky and Lark, Holly's five-month-old litter, cued Viv to invite us to accompany her on what was to be for me the first of many walks through the glen, to where Cor water meets up with Tweed. We were accompanied by the older 'Teen-agers' — Dee and her brother Glen, then their mother, Holly, and following up in the rear 'The Pensioners' — Garry and his son Laddie.

I have never felt in awe of meeting a dog before, but I must confess to experiencing this particular sentiment on being introduced to Viv's Garry, (or Sir Garry, as he came to be known later on in our relationship). I looked into his beautiful eyes which for all his years still blazed with keen intelligence, and felt that, at least, I ought to curtsy.

It is lovely to walk through the glen behind the shepherd's cottage that the Billingham's call home, but on that first day of our meeting I was so engrossed in conversation listening to the numerous anecdotes about the dogs, that I failed to notice a pair of roe deer silently disappear into the safety of the forest. Neither did I observe a shoal of young salmon flit gleefully through the shallows, or the multitude of wild flowers that blushed unseen, content to show themselves the following season to a then more receptive explorer.

The following morning Estie and I watched enraptured as Garry and Holly demonstrated their prowess to a small group of tourists. Garry has since retired and I count myself privileged to have seen him in action. I remember an American visitor standing beside me nodding with approval and telling his wife how obvious the experience of the older dog was to him.

Later, Holly accompanied us to 'The Wee School', where there is a photographic exhibition of shepherds and the dogs that brought them fame and fortune. Viv began explaining not about the photographs, but how it had come about that her hair, which had been waist-length, had all broken off — a hilarious tale. While we all fell about with laughter, I caught the expression on Holly's face. She sat absolutely still, gazing up at her mistress with what can only be described as adoration.

On the way back to the yard we observed Geoff putting Jan and Bett through their paces. His quiet manner deeply impressed me. Just a little whistle or a single word softly spoken, was all that was required. How I wish that I could have been at the Scottish National in 1986 to see them win the Brace Championship.

It was almost time to leave. Viv had to fill in a form to register my puppy. 'Have you decided on a name for her?' she asked. That morning as Estie and I drove through Tweedsmuir sight-seeing, we passed a signpost pointing to

Talla. I had recently read in a journal written by George
Burnett a description of the place as being... 'far remote
from human habitation. A small river or rather a mountain
torrent, called the Talla, breaks down the glen with great
fury, dashing successively over a number of small cascades,
which has procured the spot the name Talla Linns'.

And so she was registered Whitelaw Talla — Whitelaw
being the prefix Geoff uses and the name of one of the hills
he shepherded before he came to Tweedsmuir.

It was time to set off on the long journey home. We
popped Talla into a box lined with newspapers and after
promising to keep in touch, said our goodbyes. Our visit
had been enlightening to say the least and it had been
marvellous to observe an authentic way of life. The
extraordinary qualities of the dogs and the dedication of
their owners struck a deep chord within.

It was unfortunate that we had to return south so soon.
As we drove by the little school house, I longed to return
and learn more about an occupation that has changed little
during the past centuries.

High in the sky a tawny feathered kestrel tilted his wing to
catch the thermal. His beady eyes ever alert, missing
nothing of the interaction down below.

It is customary for most academic terms to begin in the
autumn. So it was, that Talla and I returned for a weekend's
tuition at Tweedhopefoot. That season Viv was running her
young dog Glen in the nursery trials, so on Saturday we
drove the hour and a quarter to Stow, near Galashiels,
where Alastair Cutter had set up a course. As we sped
through lovely Peeblesshire, sparkling in the morning frost,
we listened to the haunting voice of Iain Thomson, a

shepherd working on the Isle of Mull, sing his own songs which, in the title of the tape recording, he has dedicated 'To a Working Collie'.

I remember that when we arrived at our destination the light was dazzling. Looking up the field the sheep were barely distinguishable in the glare. The penetrating wind blowing into one's face increased the difficulty in spotting them. Glen ran well that day — although he didn't win a prize. Trialling is a great leveller!

This being my first introduction to trialling in Scotland it was thrilling to observe famous handlers that previously I had only read about. Viv introduced me to many of her friends, one being Dougie Lamb, who was running a young bitch called Fly. (On returning home I ordered the *Scottish Farmer*, a magazine which at least helps me to keep pace with the trial results in Scotland.)

During the day Viv explained what was required of the dogs and how they were pointed for their runs. Through observing carefully I quickly learned to recognise the difference between 'handlers' and 'class handlers' and commented on the obvious high standard compared to some of the other trials I had attended.

Meanwhile, Talla and I were still in the cradle. I first took her to see sheep when she was 12 weeks old and she had been interested right from the word go. I needed to find a local shepherd who would be able to help us get started. Eventually I was fortunate in finding Bob Wilden who lives but a stone's throw from me. Bob's first remark on meeting Talla was: 'She's very small.' To his surprise and my pleasure she immediately lowered her head, tucked in her tail and began to drive the sheep down the field, proving that 'good stuff comes in little parcels'. From then on we visited Bob regularly.

During that autumn weekend at Tweedhopefoot (Talla
was by that time around eight months old), Viv took us out
into the training paddock and told me where I was going
wrong. Both she and Geoff gave lots of good advice as well
as encouragement and suggested that I should come back
the following year. The weekend passed all too quickly and
I had to return home. It was with reluctance that I drove
past the Devil's Beeftub, through Moffat and headed south.
'Ah well, roll on next year,' I enthused as I changed gear.

High above Tweedhopefoot the kestrel soared, observing
the many changes that were taking place. He watched with
interest the two black and white collies streak down the
valley to gather the scattered flock and puzzled at the
meaning of the shepherds' shrill whistles. Lately he noted
that one of the shepherd's left the farm a little after 9am in
order to drive the 12 miles or so to Broughton, where he
collected two young men off the early bus. Ross and
Tommy were building a circular stell at Tweedhopefoot.
The kestrel swooped low, studying the boys' midday ritual
of feeding the ducks. For some reason this giving of titbits
irritated him — perhaps it was because the ducks had such
an easy time of it.
    He would rather starve than forfeit his independence.

Talla and I returned in May of the following year.
Tweedhopefoot looked spectacular, with wild flowers
growing everywhere. Outside the farm buildings tubs of
geraniums waited eagerly to bloom and a large freshly
painted red cartwheel leaned against the newly whitened
walls. The lambing was not quite finished and already
Geoff and Viv were in top gear! It wasn't until late that
evening that they were ready to hear my news.

After I returned to Suffolk I had begun shepherding full-time. All ideas of going to Portugal were shelved. There was too much to learn here — and preferably north of the Border! I had spent the winter months working for Bob Wilden, assisting at two lambings before taking another on single-handed. It turned out to be the most rewarding work I had ever undertaken. I delighted in the company of my collie and our woolly charges. The farmer came each day to feed the sheep, and at the end of lambing presented me with a black orphaned lamb and invited me back the following year. When lambing was over I joined a gang of sheep shearers and went 'wool winding'. If I thought lambing was hard work, I soon realised that I didn't know the meaning of the word!

My husband had a building job in London which was going to keep him tied-up for a couple of months. Geoff and Viv had offered me employment as well as an opportunity to train Talla and attend sheep dog trials. How could I refuse?

While the sheep dog handling demonstrations were in progress I would be putting the kettle on. There is an 'olde-worlde' charm about the Bothy, where the tables are decked with wild flowers and covered with pretty blue table-cloths set in readiness for delicious cream teas.

The tearoom provides an ideal area in which to display the crafts, the theme being 'The shepherd and his dog'. Many of the items on sale are made exclusively for Tweedhopefoot.

On Fridays, during lunchtime, we would dash to Moffat to do the weekly shopping and just as important, to post trial entries. If these were received too late they would be returned and the chance to compete forfeited, there were so many entrants.

*In the
Bothy
tearoom*

*'Talla wasn't
the problem —
it was me!'*

On Saturdays, being the only day between Easter and October that Tweedhopefoot is closed to to the public, we would set off at the crack of dawn to drive to a trial. These events are so much a part of the rural life in Scotland. Most of the courses looked more testing than those in the south — where of course the terrain is so different — and then there's the 'beer tent', always the focal point in Scotland and seldom seen in England.

This 'gathering hole' is part of the tradition, and as everyone knows, 'a wee dram keeps out the cold', especially in northern weather conditions. I found it invaluable listening to the accomplished handlers' comments and quickly realised that there is all the difference in the world between assessing a particular dog's ability on the day and knowing its real capabilities. This required regular attendance at trials as well as observing the dog in varying circumstances. Consistency being the name of the game, as well as a knowledge of breeding and the handler's own accomplishment. The more that I listened the more I realised how little I knew.

The Scottish summer evenings being long and light, provided us with an ideal opportunity to train the young dogs. So after the tearoom was closed and the last car drove out the parking area Viv would give me a session with Talla.

We used half a dozen quiet sheep in a well-fenced paddock. I had been advised by my 'teacher' that, when working with a Border collie, I should do the opposite to what my instinct told me. At the time, this advice seemed a bit of a conundrum — but it was not very long before an opportunity presented itself and the point of what she meant was clearly illustrated.

During our first training session Talla began racing

around and around the sheep and would not take a blind bit of notice when I asked her to stop. The one thought in my head was that I had to make her lie-down and listen to me. I thought that Viv would be in the same frame of mind.

Instead, she suggested that I stand perfectly still and say absolutely nothing unless Talla stopped of her own accord, and if she did, I was to immediately encourage her to continue by making a shushing sound, 'and insist on her running in the same direction so as not to give her variety of choice'. I did as instructed and at first Talla was delighted to comply. As soon as she began to slow I shushed her on, moving the sheep so that her instinct encouraged her to head. This continued throughout the whole session. Just when I was about to collapse with dizziness Viv said: 'Ask her to stand.' I did and she stopped immediately, by then more than happy to do so. I was encouraged to praise her before putting her into her kennel. The following evening we repeated the lesson and Talla proved much more amenable. Another useful comment from Viv was, 'Unless you allow a dog to make mistakes it won't understand why you are correcting it.'

Our lessons continued. Sometimes Viv would take Talla to the sheep on her own and I would watch their progress from a distance. She improved in leaps and bounds through being allowed to learn by her mistakes, and with each outing became more and more confident in her own ability. I soon came to realise that Talla was not the problem — it was me! There were occasions when, weighed down by doubt, I wondered if I would ever progress.

For a start, my reactions were far too slow. Viv, ever patient, would insist that we practise until we got it right and that we always ended a lesson on a good note. I would fall into bed with the following instructions echoing in my

head, 'Stop her — stop her ... no, no, YOU move!'
Followed by: 'Run towards her through the sheep!... you
must get her to stop on the point of balance IM-
MEDIATELY you ask her.'... 'Help your dog — get
between her and the sheep; now that was your fault!'

'Let her go or she'll lose her sheep!' 'That's good —
that's better — give her lots of praise, she's done well...
good girl Talla, well done!' 'That'll do, give her ONE clap
— don't make her big-headed — put her in her kennel.'

As the weeks passed we improved more and more, and
since returning to Suffolk (in the autumn) I can proudly
report that Talla is helping to shepherd 700 hoggs and come
the spring we'll be off lambing again. This year she will be
a real help!

There are always dogs in for training at Tweedhopefoot. I
would observe Geoff and Viv during training lessons,
noting their patience and quiet authority. So quiet in fact,
that at times I had difficulty hearing them. Once, when I
was walking around the sheep with Geoff, he told me how
he would go to the hill with Jed and Trim when he was 'up
the Bowmont', little Trim at his heels and Jed a yard or so
in front. He explained that you didn't want to be calling
loudly to your dogs because you would startle the sheep
and they would be off! On another occasion I was walking
in the glen with Talla. She was running ahead of me and I
called her back loudly. The sound was dreadful. The peace
and tranquillity which had nurtured our walk was completely shattered by the noise. I felt acutely my intrusion
imposing itself on the environment. Talla stopped in her
tracks but did not oblige. I gave an almost inaudible call
and she immediately returned to my side. I had learned that
the tone of one's voice is more important than the volume.

Geoff had said that 'Talla must know you've got that bit of steel in you — it's something that you are born with', and Viv's 'quiet but deadly', (said with tongue in cheek!) was at last beginning to sink home. With me, often the tone of voice was wrong. Shouting was merely emphasising the error.

I had also to develop a clear idea of what I wanted to do with the sheep and where I needed to position myself and my dog to achieve this. Talla was keenly enthusiastic, loving every working moment, living to please. I needed to work with sheep as much as possible, in order to learn what is commonly termed by the experts as 'sheep sense'. Timing, anticipation and speedy reaction being other invaluable qualities. Handling a dog, I quickly discovered, is an art consisting of ten per cent inspiration and ninety per cent perspiration!

A kestrel winging his way silently down the glen heard a shout. The deer sprang in fear, sending clods of earth tumbling into the burn, startling the salmon fry. The kestrel stiffened momentarily, before flying on to find a suitable roost. In the morning he would encounter the shepherd, along the Broughton road.

One morning Geoff arrived back from Broughton, where he had gone as usual to collect Ross and Tommy, the stone-wallers. He had been driving along the road when a kestrel flew straight into the path of the car. He quickly pulled into the side and hurried back to pick up the motionless hawk. As he bent down, he noticed a tiny shrew clutched tightly in its talons. When Geoff picked up the bird it released its hold on the shrew and the little creature scampered away unharmed to the safety of the bracken.

The kestrel was stunned but fortunately still alive. Ross

held it gently in his lap on the journey back to the farm. When they arrived it was beginning to come round so Geoff carried it down to the stell, marvelling all the while at its beauty. He opened his hands to release it. The kestrel gazed curiously up at him, its head titled to one side. It shook itself, stretched its strong wings and soared straight up into the sky — higher and higher it flew until it became a mere speck. It hung there for a moment before gracefully gliding to earth, then, after circling the men below in thanks, flew swiftly down the valley.

*

It is not unheard of for some puppies to turn their homes upside down. Mine turned my life upside down! As a friend from South Africa said when we met up at Tweedhopefoot during the summer months: 'If you own a Border collie you must expect your life to change.' How right she was — my life has been incalculably enriched through owning Talla. I have undertaken projects that hitherto I would never have dreamed of, let alone taken on. She continues to grow into an intelligent dog; long-legged, medium-coated and cock-lugged, with the symmetrical facial markings of her ancestors. I handle her regularly, encouraged by Viv's guiding influence — 'driving' with her long steady distances, remembering to keep up the momentum. not giving her too much flanking, always endeavouring to be in the right position to push her off the corners of the flock, while at the same time whispering, 'Keep.' Obviously I still have an awful lot of practising to do in order to memorise the whistles, especially 'the sweet little whistle' that Geoff uses, and the clear arc Viv conveys when giving a right-hand flank — 'Ahhhwaay!'.

Yes, all of the upheaval and change of plans, not to mention jobs, has been well worth the effort. Through Talla I have come to meet and make friends with some wonderful people, as well as travelling to some beautiful places, where, instead of being treated like a tourist, I have been welcomed as a friend.

I hope that this is not the end of 'my story' concerning the farm at the foot of the Tweed. Without Viv and Geoff, their hard work and tremendous sense of humour, none of what I have related would have been possible. I personally cannot thank them enough for their friendship, kindness and their combined encouragement.

The great river of time was calling the kestrel and the year to its close. Winter, riding over the hills in all its savagery, brought gales and fierce blizzards. The kestrel, exhausted and battered by the fierce winds, chose the shelter of 'The Wee School' for its final resting place.

Beneath Death's icy shroud his spirit flows, singing its eternal song of freedom.

I see what was and is, and will abide;
Still glides the stream, and shall forever glide.

Glossary

BARE-SKINNED: Short haired.

BRACE PAIR: Two dogs working together.

CROSS-DRIVE: Driving sheep across the front of the handler in a straight line.

DRAFT EWE: A ewe that is too old for the hill.

DRIVE: When the dog takes the sheep away from the handler.

EYE: An hypnotic stare with which the dog fixes the sheep.

FANK: Square sheep pens.

FETCH: When the dog brings the sheep towards the handler.

FLANKING: When the dog runs either to the right or to the left around the sheep.

HAUGH: The valley bottom.

HOGG: A young sheep between one year old and its first shearing.

IN-BYE: Lowland fields.

LINE UP: When the dog brings the sheep in a straight line to the handler without commands.

MINDRUM: The name of the farm where the late Bob Fraser worked as a shepherd and the title of his prefix.

MULE: A cross-bred sheep sired by a Blue-faced Leicester ram out of a Swaledale ewe.

OUTRUN: The course taken by the dog when gathering the sheep.

PULLING WOOL: Mild grip.

SHED: When one or more sheep are separated from the flock by the dog.

SHUSH: Noise made by the shepherd to encourage the dog quickly around the sheep.

SOURHOPE: A research hill farm in the Bowmont Valley.

SHUTTLE GOB: See undershot.

STELL: Stone-built round sheep holding enclosure.

TACKETTY-BOOTS: Boots with rows of tacketts or mettle studs to give the wearer a better grip.

TAKE TIME: Command to go slowly.

TUP: A ram.

UNDERSHOT: When the lower jaw is shorter than the upper.

The British Sheep Dog Association was founded at Tweedhopefoot in January, 1990.

It is the Association's intention to promote sheep dogs, shepherding skills and sheep dog trials in a practical and caring manner.

There will be an annual subscription of £10. An attractively designed badge, sticker and Christmas newsletter will be provided and free access given to members at BSDA trials.

An advisory service is available for problem collies to BSDA members. Please send a stamped self-addressed envelope to:

**The British Sheep Dog Association,
Tweedhopefoot,
Tweedsmuir,
Peeblesshire,
ML12 6QS,
Scotland.
Tel: Tweedsmuir (08997) 267**